Contents

INTRODUCTION

WALK

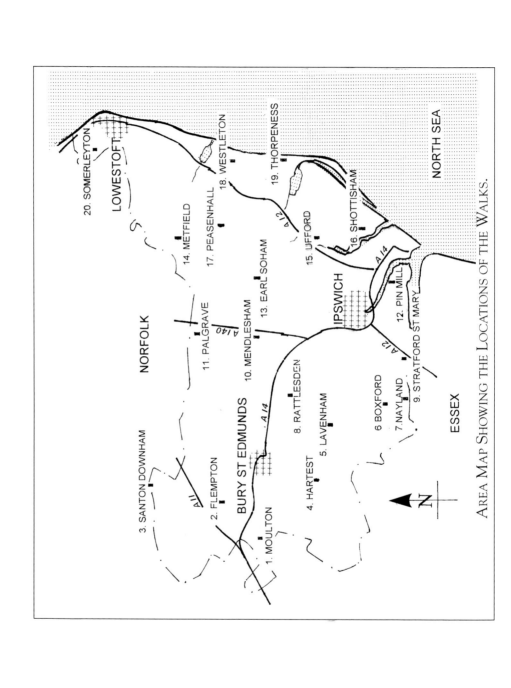

AREA MAP SHOWING THE LOCATIONS OF THE WALKS.

WALK

Publisher's Note

We hope that you obtain considerable enjoyment from this book; great care has been taken in its preparation. Although at the time of publication all routes followed public rights of way or permitted paths, diversion orders can be made and permissions withdrawn.

We cannot of course be held responsible for such diversion orders and any inaccuracies in the text which result from these or any other changes to the routes nor any damage which might result from walkers trespassing on private property. We are anxious though that all details covering the walks are kept up to date and would therefore welcome information from readers which would be relevant to future editions.

Introduction

Suffolk villages are often hidden away from the main network of county roads so a conscious effort has to be made to seek them out, but how rewarding that can be.

These walks, wide-ranging over the county, start from 20 charming and varied Suffolk villages. When in each village do also wander around the roads in the centre and those radiating out a little way, to explore other attractive features.

The county has many types of terrain, from the sandy heaths of the north-west known as the Brecks – the rolling grasslands around Newmarket where raising racehorses is a way of life – to the heavy clay land of central Suffolk, often called High Suffolk. In the east, along a broad coastal band, is another sandy, heathy area called the Sandlings. All provide good walking countryside, with a great variety of plant, animal and bird life.

Rivers also provide a focal point for several walks. The coast line is much cut by river estuaries: by the river Waveney in the north where it forms much of the northern boundary of Suffolk, by the Blythe, the Alde, the Butley river, the Deben, the Orwell and the Stour. The Stour forms the southern boundary of Suffolk for very many miles, from Shotley peninsula, past Sudbury and on towards Haverhill in the west.

Stone houses are few and far between, but there is plenty of brick, both red and Suffolk white brick, and in the north of the county particularly, flint is much used. All the villages in this book have attractive examples of local building design at its best.

Many villages have village signs, and the events or items depicted invariably give clues to parts of the village history. A few of these are explained in the book. Can you resolve some of the others?

Small villages seldom have car parks so parking can sometimes be a problem. Please park carefully and avoid obstructing the life of the village. In the book we have tried to indicate suitable parking places. Remember that modern agricultural machinery is often very large, needing lots of room when on the move. Pubs invariably have parking for their customers. Many will agree to cars being left there while you walk, but it is a good idea to ask the landlord before doing so.

In some of the villages there is more than one place to eat. One, or sometimes more, have been mentioned, but that is not meant to imply that you might not find others satisfactory! We have visited and can recommend at least one of the eating establishments mentioned in each walk. Phone numbers have been included so that opening times can be verified. 'Open all day' is not meant to be taken literally, but roughly means from about 11 am to late evening. Some pubs do not open, or do not serve meals, on some occasions; these are indicated in the text. Where meals are served dogs should be left outside.

Except where it is indicated that Permissive Paths are used, the walks are along Public Rights of Way. Such paths should be free of obstruction from vegetation and kept clear of growing crops. However, at some seasons of the year paths can become overgrown, particularly if they are not well used.

The roads are mostly lightly

trafficked highways, nevertheless please take care on country roads and generally walk facing the on-coming traffic. Stout footwear is recommended. All unsurfaced paths can be muddy and wet at times.

The sketch maps, not to scale, are intended to illustrate the route. Not every item of detail has been depicted. For those requiring more detail, the relevant OS Landranger 1:50,000 map numbers are given.

Please respect the countryside observing the Country Code:

Enjoy the countryside and respect its life and work.
Guard against all risk of fire.
Fasten all gates.
Keep your dogs under close control.
Keep to public paths across farmland.

Use gates and stiles to cross fences, hedges and walls.
Leave livestock, crops and machinery alone.
Take your litter home.
Help to keep all water clean.
Protect wildlife, plants and trees.
Take special care on country roads.
Make no unnecessary noise.

We would like to thank Suffolk County Council's Rights-of-Way staff throughout the County for their help.

We hope you enjoy discovering Suffolk's lovely villages and have many interesting and satisfying walks using them as your base.

Have a nice day!

Jean and Geoff Pratt

MOULTON

Length: 4 miles

Getting there: Moulton is 4 miles east of Newmarket, and just south of Kentford. From the east, leave the A14 at the slip road towards Newmarket (B1506). In 1½ miles turn left on the B1085. Otherwise go to Newmarket and follow the	B1506 towards Bury St Edmunds. Turn right at Kentford on the B1085. At Moulton, turn left for the packhorse bridge and the start. **Parking:** There is room for several cars at the roadside,	beside a high wall, on Brookside, a minor road running south from the packhorse bridge. The King's Head has a customers' car park. **Map:** OS Landranger 154 Cambridge (GR 697645).

Moulton, at the western edge of Suffolk, lies on chalky downland and its proximity to Newmarket means that the breeding, care and training of horses are major activities in the area. Horses often graze on the large green at the heart of the village.

Running through the green is the river Kennett which flows northwards to join the Lark, a tributary of the Great Ouse.

Besides the 15th century four-arch packhorse bridge, at one end of the green, there is another old flint bridge on the way

FOOD and DRINK

The King's Head public house is close by the old packhorse bridge. It is open, serving food, every day except Monday, unless it is a Bank Holiday. Generous helpings of chicken Maryland, steak and kidney pie, King's Head grill, King's Todger and fresh salmon steaks can be obtained. Banana longboat, sticky toffee pudding, baked Alaska, Honeymoon Heave and more could follow. Telephone: 01638 750156.

to St Peter's church. The green is flanked by many delightful old buildings, including the Rectory School of 1849. Beautiful flint walls abound in the village.

It is over those two bridges that the walk begins, taking you south out of the village and alongside the river Kennett. Climbing up to Gazeley, there is the opportunity to see 14th-century All Saints' church. The Gazeley Stud is nearby. There are lovely views over the countryside at many points during the walk, before the return to Moulton.

THE WALK

❶ From the ancient packhorse bridge go south, taking the stony track following the stream on your left. Go left across the Old Flint Bridge, with its flint faced parapet, to the road and turn right beside the tall flint

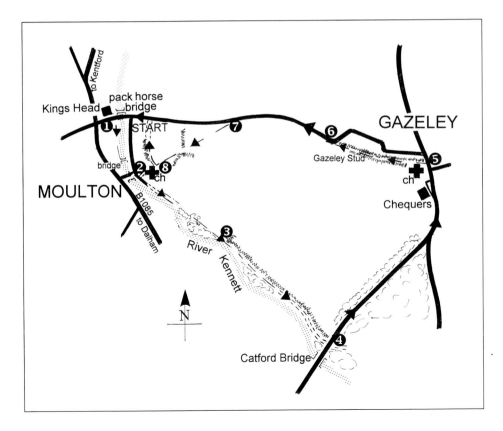

Moulton's 15th-century packhorse bridge.

wall. Keep along the road, ignoring roads which cross the river by ford or bridge.

❷ Pass on the left a lane to the church, which stands on a hill. Continue straight along a grassy cart track beside the river. The cart track soon ends at a field. Continue along a path between a fence on the left and a small wooded area on the right. After going through a little wood, swing out to a field and continue along a headland path with at first, a hedge, and later a wood, on the right.

❸ At the end of the field there is a cross-hedge on the left, and here the path is almost on the bank of the river Kennett. Keep straight on along a cart track with the wooded bank of the river on the right. As the

path diverges gradually from the river, pass a young plantation on the right, and further on the track becomes a wider gravel road.

❹ Come out to a road and turn left, climbing a hill beside a fine band of beeches about 50 yards wide on the left.

PLACES of INTEREST

Newmarket is only 4 miles away and there, in the High Street, is the **National Horse Racing Museum.** You can tack up a model horse, dress up in silks, before weighing out and riding a horse simulator. It is open daily except Mondays from March till the end of October, and in July and August and on Bank Holidays it is also open on Mondays. The licensed café and shop are open throughout the year, except Christmas and the first week in January. Telephone: 01638 667333.

On the right there is mixed woodland. Join a road coming in on the right and enter Gazeley. In ¼ mile pass the Chequers public house and reach All Saints' church.

❺ Immediately after the churchyard turn left at a sign and walk through the edge of the churchyard. Go out through a kissing gate and follow a broad footpath between immaculately trimmed hedges, beside the paddocks of the Gazeley Stud. Note the fine weatherboarded barn on the right.

After passing the paddocks the path comes out along a headland with a hedge continuing on the right. Very soon come out to a road at a bend. There is a water tower about 200 yards away on the right.

❻ Keep straight on along the road. In just under ½ mile, the road makes a slight bend to the right and starts to descend into the valley.

❼ Shortly, at a footpath sign, leave the road, going left through the hedge. Walk diagonally across this field to a corner and go out over a stile. There are fine views to right and left.

Continue on the well-walked path passing the end of a hedge on the left, but gradually getting further and further away from it. On the far side of this field cross a stile and drop steeply down through some woods, to a stile in the churchyard wall at Moulton.

❽ Do not enter the churchyard but turn right before the stile. At first the churchyard wall is on the left, but later there is a hedge. Keep on the path in the same direction and pass some stables. Go through a pedestrian gate beside an iron gate and continue along a concrete drive to a road. Turn left to return to the packhorse bridge and the start.

FLEMPTON

Length: 6 miles (or 4½ miles)

Getting there: Exit the A14 at the junction for Bury West. Follow the B1106 for Fornham All Saints and turn left on to the A1101. Reach Flempton in 2 miles and turn right for the village.	Parking: By the churchyard wall there is room for one or two cars. There is a customers' car park at the Greyhound public house close by the church, and also a small layby	on the A1101 at the edge of the village. Map: OS Landranger 155 Bury St Edmunds, (GR 812699).

The village lies just north of the A1101 Bury St Edmunds to Wisbech road, at the crossroads by the flint-faced church. An attractive pink-washed house under a plain-tiled roof, a terrace of thatched white cottages, and the one-time forge, part hidden in the trees, form an attractive picture around the green.

The Lark Valley in which Flempton lies runs through the area called the Brecks, which covers about 400 square miles of mainly sandy heathland. In nearby Icklingham in 1877 were discovered hundreds of Roman silver coins, dating from the last century of Roman rule in Britain.

FOOD and DRINK

The Greyhound is a pleasant, well-cared-for pub, with several dining areas and an enclosed garden where children are safe. The choice of food is wide: for instance, you could have whole smoked trout, home-made beef chilli and taco shells, or escalope of pork cordon bleu. Apple pie and chocolate fudge cake are just two of the sweets. Open seven days a week. Telephone: 01284 728400.

This interesting walk crosses the river Lark and then follows the pretty Lark Valley Path through Culford Park. There is a fine view of Culford Hall, and walking through the Park you will pass a magnificent cast-iron bridge over the lake. This historic bridge was designed, probably by Samuel Wyatt, in 1803. It has recently been rediscovered, hidden deep in reeds and undergrowth, in this former estate of Lord Cornwallis which since 1935 has been home to Culford School. The walk continues across farmland to the edge of the Kings Forest to return through the tiny village of West Stow, passing the Hall with its Tudor gatehouse.

THE WALK

❶ Walk away from the main road, passing the green on the left and follow West Stow Road to cross, in 200 yards, a bridge. Soon take a narrow hump-backed bridge over the river Lark and bend to the right. Ignore a minor road to the right. At a T-junction, opposite a drive to Culford School flanked by two flint lodges, turn left.

❷ Pass Cornwallis Close and just beyond it, turn right at a sign 'Lark Valley Path'.

Walk the narrow path for a few yards and soon turn left on to a surfaced drive close to a lily-covered lake. Very shortly, pass an overflow weir to the lake. In about 100 yards look out for a waymark on a post beside the drive. At this point, go right along a narrow permissive footpath signed 'Lark Valley Path', skirting the lake.

Bend round to the left, following the lake and in a little over ¼ mile, come to an ornamental bridge. Keep straight on beside the lake. Half-left is a fine view of Culford Hall.

At a waymark, about 150 yards before the end of the lake, turn left on a narrow path away from the water. Turn right at a track at right-angles and follow it round in an arc to the left. On the left is Culford church.

❸ The track joins a surfaced drive. Turn right and follow it along an avenue of Wellingtonias, walk out through recently refurbished iron gates and turn left along the road for 300 yards.

❹ Enter, left, the school drive, signed to the church. Keep on the main drive as it bends right and then left. When the tall wall on the left ends, at a road junction with a central grassy triangle, find a footpath sign. Here go right. The official map shows the footpath crossing the playing field. However, go along a drive beside the playing field.

After passing all the buildings on the right, turn left at the end of the drive, skirting the playing field. Just beyond the last games pitch and a few yards from a large beech tree on the left, go right through a tree belt.

The magnificent cast-iron bridge in Culford Park.

❺ Leave the trees and continue on a grassy cart track. Pass a brick water tower and continue straight on to the B1106 Brandon to Bury road.

Anyone wishing to make a short cut should go left along the road, and where the B1106 turns right, keep straight on. In ¼ mile bend left at Brickfield Farm and rejoin the walk at ❽.

Continuing the main walk, turn right along this busy road.

❻ Where the main road bends to the right, with a minor road straight on, go left on a concrete farm road, which in a few yards becomes a well-used stony lane between hedges. Pass the end of Lime Kiln Plantation and in ¼ mile, at the end of the field on the left and where the track you have been following continues with

hedges on both sides, go left on a grassy cart track with a small wood on the right.

In 50 yards keep straight on across an open field, on the far side of which pass Blake's Spinney, and later a stand of newly planted trees on the left. At a hedge, go right for 2 yards, then left through the hedge and continue straight on along another cart track. Go through a gap in a thin hedge and continue as before. Half-left can be seen the now redundant church of All Saints Wordwell.

❼ Eventually reach a road. Cross straight over and go towards Wordwell Hall. With a large modern barn on the right, and before reaching the Hall, go left at a footpath sign, along a cart track through a field. At the corner of the Hall garden the route continues, bearing slightly right.

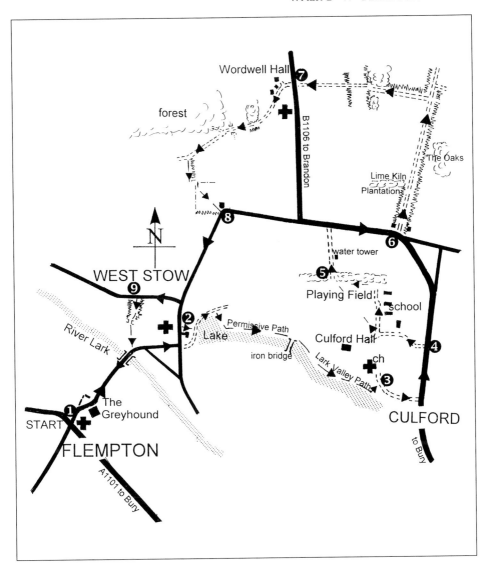

Go through a gate, passing a wood on the right. Continue straight on, through another gate into a field, then in about 50 yards cross a culvert over a shallow ditch. In accordance with the waymark, bear half-left, still following a cart track.

Go over a stile beside a gate and imme-diately turn left, leaving the track. Cross a ditch by a culvert and in the corner of a field, go over a stile, turn right and enter the next field. Cross the field diagonally to a stile beside a gap at the field corner.

❽ Walk out to a road opposite Brickfield

PLACES of INTEREST

West Stow Anglo-Saxon Village is only a mile away and it gives a fascinating insight into life in those times. The West Stow Country Park covers 125 acres. The entrance to the reconstructed village is through the Visitor Centre, which has many displays and a video. Those who visit the village may take around with them an audio guide. There are often special events and demonstrations; there are pigs and hens, and sometimes there are 'Anglo-Saxon' people in costume to chat to you. The Visitor Centre and Village are open daily from 10 am to 5 pm. Telephone: 01284 728718. (No dogs allowed in the village.) **Lackford Wildfowl Reserve** (TL802706) is 1 mile west of Flempton. Turn off the A1101 at the brown sign, and follow the track to the Reserve. At these restored gravel pits you may expect to see wildfowl and waders. There are two hides.

Farm and go right along the road. When you get to a road junction turn right, signed 'Saxon Village'. There is a footway along this road. Soon you will be walking beside a flint wall on the right.

❾   About 30 yards before a 'Beware of Deer' road sign come to a stile at a gap in a wall. West Stow Hall is barely 150 yards further on, set well back from the road. It has a large Tudor gatehouse with onion-top turrets. A Tudor brick porch, with rooms above, links the gatehouse to the house itself.

Having glimpsed West Stow Hall, retrace your steps to the gap in the wall, cross the stile and continue along a narrow lane, between trees. Shortly the lane bears round to the right and leads to a substantial footbridge with masonry parapets. Cross a stile and go straight across a rough pasture, passing a magnificent oak tree about 10 yards away on the left.

Go through a gap at the right-hand end of a rough masonry wall which leads to the road to Flempton. Turn right, back to the start.

SANTON DOWNHAM

Length: 5 miles (or 1½ miles)

Getting there: Santon Downham is 2½ miles east of Brandon at the northern edge of Suffolk. From a roundabout on the A11, on the Thetford Bypass, take the B1107 towards	Brandon and in 2½ miles fork right to reach the village in a mile. **Parking:** There is a large car park, with toilets, in front of the	Thetford Forest Park Headquarters just by the village shop. **Map:** OS Landranger 144 Thetford (GR 816877).

The oldest part of Santon Downham is nearest to the river, where you will pass a long terrace of single-storey flint cottages with trim gardens. Under the soil are vast quantities of flints, making them a major local building material. They were mined hereabouts as long as 4,000 years ago (see Grimes Graves in Places of Interest box).

A small church, called The Church in the Forest, faces the green. A church here was mentioned in the Domesday Book of 1086.

Santon Downham is in the middle of the area called Breckland. The Brecks cover 400 square miles of vast heaths and arable fields, with much of it given over to

❷ In 200 yards go left along a gravel Forest Ride (No 17). Soon after reaching a field on the left, pass a footpath through a Forest Ride on the right, and in about 50 yards come to a track off to the left.

Anyone wishing to take the short (1½ mile) walk should turn left along this track for 150 yards to cross the Little Ouse river and continue to the St Helen's car park and picnic area, rejoining the walk at ❾.

❸ For the main walk, go straight on along the forest track still following the Little

forestry, mainly pine, since the 1920s. Many of the houses were built for forestry workers, but few people in the village today work for the Forestry Commission.

The Romans introduced rabbits to this area for both their meat and fur. Sheep have grazed on these light soils since time immemorial. The soil is so light that sand-blows occur from time to time. In 1668 a particularly disastrous one engulfed this small village, when it was described as a sand-flood.

A woodland track takes you into part of the Thetford Forest, following the Little Ouse Path. This is a lovely peaceful walk of woods and water. On the return, along part of the Hereward Way you pass St Helen's Well, deep and tree-lined, before it is time to return to Santon Downham.

THE WALK

❶ From the Forestry car park go out to the road and turn right. Pass St Mary's church on the left. Then joining a road coming in on the right, swing left, following the signs for the Little Ouse Path.

Part of the Little Ouse Path.

Ouse Path. Eventually pass Forest Ride 20 and keep straight on along the same sandy track.

❹ In about ¼ mile, when directly ahead about 200 yards away, you can see a grassy field, turn right off the track at a waymark and a footpath sign nailed high up on a pine tree. Although well-used, this footpath through the woods is in sharp contrast to the track that has been used so far, being much narrower. In about 100 yards cross straight over a wide cart track leading to a farm and continue on a broad sandy track which soon becomes a grassy way between fields, following a fence on the left.

❺ At the corner of the field go left as waymarked, keeping beside the fence on the left. In 200 yards, at the next corner, follow the fence round half-left and in a few yards go right on a narrow footpath across a newly planted area of conifers.

At the far side of the new plantation, turn right along a grassy track gently climbing beside the trees on the left. Near the top of the hill you come to a fire break about 100 yards wide, free of trees, stretching left and right.

❻ On the far side, turn left at a waymark, following the Ouse Valley Path along a pleasant cart track. At the end of the fire break go straight on and drop down a steep bank to a poplar plantation on a path which leads directly to a bridge over the river. Immediately after the bridge go right along the river bank.

Continue beside the Little Ouse and at

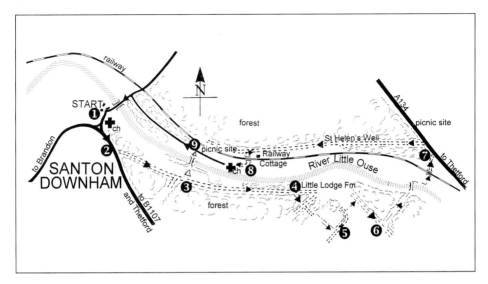

a timber slipway signed 'Breckland District Scouts' go left away from the river and head for a bridge under the railway. After the bridge, cross a steel stile and follow the track to the A134 road from Thetford.

❼ Go left for about 100 yards. Almost opposite a Forestry picnic site, leave the road, going left along a gravel track signed '21'. This is the Hereward Way. After about ½ mile you come to another sign reading '21'. At this point look down into a deep tree-lined area on the left. According to the map it is St Helen's Well and the site of St Helen's Oratory.

Keep straight on for about ½ mile and after passing Railway Cottages on the left, turn left at a junction and go under the railway line.

❽ Immediately afterwards swing right towards All Saints' church and the few dwellings which comprise the tiny village of Santon. At the church join a surfaced road. Soon on the right there is St Helen's picnic area.

❾ From the car park, keep straight on along the surfaced road. In a little over ½ mile, turn left at the T-junction and shortly cross the Little Ouse, in about 100 yards returning to the start of the walk.

HARTEST

Length: 5 miles (or 4 miles)

Getting there: Hartest is 8 miles south of Bury St Edmunds on the B1066 road, which runs between the A143 near Horringer and the	A1092 near Long Melford. **Parking:** The village car park is just west of the green, off the	road to Somerton. **Map:** OS Landranger 155 Bury St Edmunds (GR 834524).

Hartest lies in a cup in the hills; all roads out of the village climb upwards to the rim. Central to Hartest is a large triangular green. The church, surrounded by trees, and the Crown public house occupy most of the south side. The Institute, several houses and farms line the road on the west side, but a good deal of the village life seems to take place along the eastern side,

where old houses of many styles, one or two shops and an old chapel face the edge of the green.

The Hartest Local History Group has researched and published 'A *Village History*'. In it, with some hilarity, they recount how the Hartest Stone which lies on the green was brought down in 1713 to the village, and the course of events when

FOOD and DRINK

The Crown, a spacious and very old inn at the southern end of the green, serves grilled steak, deep-fried cod, haddock or plaice, ricotta and spinach cannelloni in a provençal sauce and a selection of vegetarian dishes. It is open every day of the week, serving food at both lunchtime and evening. Telephone: 01284 830250. There are Tea Rooms at Gifford's Hall (see Places of Interest box).

that glacial erratic was found in a neighbouring village. If you enjoy your day in Hartest you will want to read the book.

Climbing out of Hartest, the walk takes you through rolling farmland and beside woods to Chadacre Park. Fine views are an added bonus, and the return winds through more lovely open countryside to bring you back to Hartest village.

THE WALK

❶ Starting on the southern side of the village green, outside the Crown, take the road passing the church on the right. Leave the green, cross the bridge and turn left at the junction, along the road signed Lawshall. Pass Green View on the right and in just under 200 yards, where the road bends left, go right at a grassy triangle along a No Through Road.

❷ In ¼ mile bear left at a footpath sign along a leafy lane. Where a track swings right to a house, continue straight on, climbing a sunken lane. Soon after the end of the lane turn left beside the hedge on the left.

❸ At a corner turn right along a hard farm road. In 100 yards or so leave the track and go left over a stile and straight

across a pasture to cross another stile. Continue with a hedge on the left through a grassy field to a third stile and go straight on.

Pass through a fence and then continue on a grassy ride beside a wood on the right. At the corner of the wood keep along the track which swings half-left and then through a cross-hedge to continue as a wide path beside a hedge on the right.

❹ Just before the track swings round to the left, at a waymark, go right through a slim gap along a narrow footpath. Continue beside a stream on the left. When you come to a brick bridge go left over the stream and then almost immediately, at a waymark, go right.

The official path is straight across the field, gradually getting further away from the river on the right. Make for a waymark at the far side of the field and about 75 yards to the left of the river. However, if the path is not clear, people seem to follow the river bank and then the field edge to reach the waymarked route.

At the far side of the field cross the ditch and immediately turn left, and then continue on a narrow headland path. Later, follow the hedge and at the ranch-

PLACES of INTEREST

Gifford's Hall is a 33 acre vineyard and much more. Take the road up Hartest Hill and follow the brown signs from the B1066. There are wildflower meadows to be explored, black St Kilda sheep and black Berkshire pigs to see. Visit the rose garden, the organic vegetable garden and the sweet peas grown under cover. Maybe finish your visit with a cream tea. Open daily from 11 am to 6 pm from Easter to the end of October. Telephone: 01284 830464.

Part of the village green with the Hartest Stone in the foreground.

style fence, with a fine barn conversion building ahead, go right at a waymark.

❺ Come out to a road at Audley End and turn right. Keep along the road for just over ½ mile. Where a wood on the right ends, turn right at a bridleway sign along a surfaced drive through Chadacre Park, formerly an agricultural college. Go downhill and at the valley bottom cross the Chad Brook on a bridge with brick parapets.

❻ From the bridge walk straight ahead on a broad cart track with, at first, fences on both sides and then a hedge on the right. In the far corner of the field go out to a concrete farm road opposite a white-painted house.

❼ Go left for ¼ mile along the farm road and pass on the left a quaint brick tower.

❽ At a junction about 100 yards beyond the tower, take the left-hand track going towards some black barns. Just before the gate, go right through a narrow timber crush and take a well-walked cross-field path towards the corner of the hedge at the top of the hill. At the hedge go through the gap and then continue on a grassy headland path with a rising bank on the left. Note half-right a fine view of Hartest. Before long, skirt round beside a chalet-bungalow to reach a road.

For the short cut, turn right along the road, down a steep hill and back to the green at Hartest about 300 yards away.

To continue the 5 mile walk, turn left and pass on the right thatched, white Pippin Cottage. Note as you pass, an ancient AA sign on the side of a timber garage.

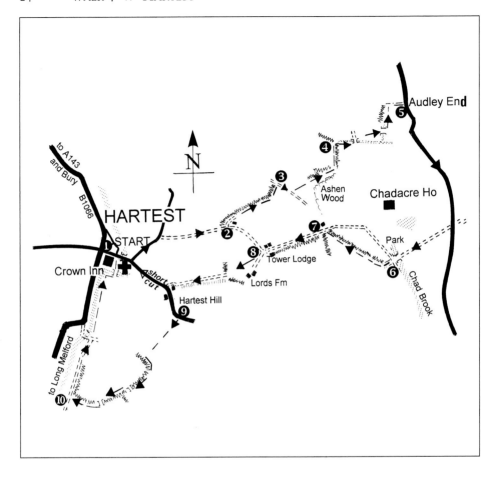

❾ After passing a letterbox turn right at a footpath sign opposite Elizel's Cottage, and take a well-walked cross-field path. At the field boundary go left and follow the hedge on the right, which soon sweeps round to the right. You are on a well maintained broad grassy headland. About 50 yards before a field boundary, at a waymark go right across a culvert and then continue with a hedge on the left. At another waymark go left and re-cross the ditch on the left and then turn right across a sleeper bridge. The path continues, again with a hedge on the right.

❿ On meeting a stony cart track at right angles go right, crossing a large culvert and continue with a hedge on the right. At the end of the field go straight on with a plantation of mixed trees on the left. Soon the track skirts a stream on the left. When you meet a gravel track, keep straight on. Later ignore a footbridge crossing the river on the left and continue straight on. The path makes a sharp turn to the right and shortly swings left by a timber fence. Turn left over the stream at a footbridge and then walk straight out to the road by the village green and the start.

LAVENHAM

Length: 6 miles (or 3 miles)

Getting there: Lavenham is 4 miles north-east of Long Melford. From Bury St Edmunds, take the A134 towards Sudbury and turn off onto the A1141 to reach Lavenham in about 4 miles. Otherwise follow the A1141 from Hadleigh.

Parking: There is parking in the Market Place. A public car park is situated beyond the Angel, just off Prentice Street. Another one is not far from the church (observe the signs).

Map: OS Landranger 155 Bury St Edmunds (GR 916493).

There can be no village in Suffolk with as many old and attractive buildings as Lavenham, all carefully preserved and many of them listed. The Guildhall, built in the early part of the 16th century, almost fills one long side of the Market Place. On another side is 14th century Little Hall, timber-framed and ochre-washed, housing the Gayer Anderson collection.

Lavenham was an important centre of the wool and cloth trade, and the merchants who dealt in those commodities became rich and built themselves fine houses. Besides the High Street explore Prentice, Bolton, Shilling, Barn, Lady and superb character to the wealth and generosity of the wool merchants.

The delights of Lavenham are complemented by this enjoyable walk. Pleasant country footpaths follow a shallow valley, leading to a tributary of the river Brett at the charming old village of Brent Eleigh with its ancient church. Returning along a green lane on higher ground above the river, you have a glorious view of Lavenham church dominating the surrounding area. There is a shorter alternative, leaving out Brent Eleigh.

Water Streets, and see the variety of wonderfully preserved and colourful buildings. The magnificent church of St Peter and St Paul, whose 141 foot tower dominates the surrounding countryside, stands at Lavenham's southern edge. It, too, owes its

THE WALK

❶ From the square, face away from the Angel and leave the square along narrow Market Lane, which curves down to the High Street. Turn left, and opposite the

Corner Farm, Brent Eleigh.

Greyhound turn right along Hall Road. About 50 yards before the road bends right, go left at a footpath sign. After crossing a stream, go right-ish, through a meadow towards Lavenham church. Enter the churchyard, keep left round the church and walk between clipped box bushes out to the road.

❷ Turn left and walk down the hill. Turn right at a junction by some half-timbered cottages, along Bear's Lane. Pass a road off to the right and keep straight on.

❸ In about 100 yards the housing on the right ends. Leaving the road, take the footpath parallel to the road, with the roadside hedge on your left. Pass a field corner beside the road, but keep straight on. At the field boundary, go into the next field and turn left, following a ditch on the left.

❹ Returning to the road, go right. Pass Weaner's Farm on the right and immediately before some barns on the left, go left at a footpath sign. Skirt round the barn, and then behind Bear's Lane Farmhouse. Swing round to the right along a headland path which, after a cross hedge, meets a cart track at the corner of a pond. Here go left beside a hedge on the left for about 100 yards to a three-way junction of footpaths.

At this point, for the short cut back to Lavenham, go left, with the hedge on the left, downhill to a road and turn right. Walk along the main road, pass a track on the left and about 50 yards before the bridge with white painted rails go left over a gate, as signed, and walk across a

meadow towards Lavenham church's distant tower. Cross a track and follow the stream on the right. At a field boundary cross a stile into a camping ground and continue beside the stream. Continue beyond the recreation ground out to a road, then turn right at a junction. In 100 yards rejoin the main walk.

❺ The full walk continues straight on along the cart track beside the hedge. At a cross-hedge turn right along the track, now with a hedge on the right. At the valley bottom go left.

❻ In 100 yards, where the main track bends right to Abbot's Hall, go straight on along a farm track. In 50 yards follow a wide grassy path with a ditch on the left and a plantation of poplars beyond it.

Pass a small pond on the right and continue on this pleasant grassy track, stream on the left and plantation on the right. Soon the route is through a leafy poplar grove. Later follow a blackthorn hedge on

---

PLACES of INTEREST

The Guildhall (National Trust) has displays of local history, farming, industry and the development of the railway. There is an exhibition of 700 years of the medieval wool cloth trade. Dye plants are still grown in the walled garden behind. Open from March till November, daily except Good Friday, from 11 am to 5 pm. Telephone: 01787 247646. **Little Hall**, hard by the Market Place, is a 14th century hall-house with a beautiful garden, and also the headquarters of the Suffolk Preservation Society. Open to the public from Easter till October, afternoons, on Wednesday, Thursday, Saturday, Sunday and Bank Holiday Mondays. Telephone: 01787 247179.

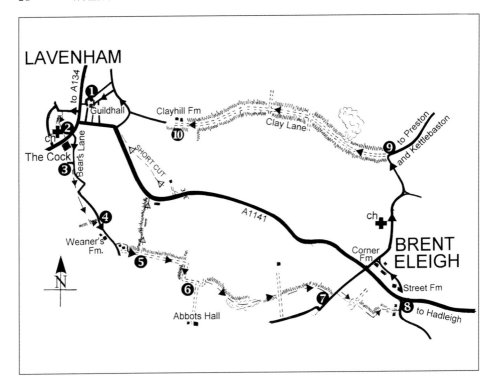

the right, and soon reach a concrete farm drive leading to Hill Farm on the left. Go right for 10 yards and then turn left on a grassy headland with a mature hedge on the left, behind which you may glimpse a lake. Follow the valley bottom round to the right.

❼ On reaching a road, Cock Lane, turn left. At the top of the hill turn right over a stile and cross a field, keeping parallel with the fence on the right. On the far side of the field find a gap in the fence, and take a path through a small wood. Pass a lane to the left and a wooded Suffolk Wildlife Trust site to the right. Keep straight on along a headland path, with a hedge on the left.

Keep beside the hedge for several bends and, about 20 yards from a corner, swing left at a waymark and follow the narrow footpath down between hedges, then some steps to the road. Turn left.

❽ In about 200 yards cross the main road into the head of a cul-de-sac at Brent Eleigh. Keep along the road and pass Colman's Cottages, a fine brick terrace. At the three-way junction, by attractive half-timbered Corner Farm, turn right, cross the river bridge and climb 300 yards to St Mary's church. Continue up the narrow road for ¼ mile towards Preston and Kettlebaston, passing a road to Monks Eleigh.

❾ Where the road makes a sharp turn to the right, go left at a bridleway sign along Clay Lane. This pleasant lane is decked in spring with primroses, anemones and violets. Keep straight on along the lane for about 1¼ miles passing woods, orchards and fields. See a marvellous view of Lavenham church tower dominating the whole village.

❿ Pass Clayhill farmhouse on the right and descend a surfaced road into a shallow valley. Cross a river-bridge with white handrails and at a T-junction turn right, keeping the river on the right. (This is where the short-cut rejoins the main walk.)

In 300 yards, go left up Bolton Street. On the right is half-timbered High Hall, and other interesting houses. At the end of Bolton Street go right passing ochre-washed Little Hall and in 50 yards enter the square, back to the start.

Market Place, Lavenham, with Little Hall shown on the right of the picture.

BOXFORD

Length: 5 miles

Getting there: Boxford is half-way between Sudbury and Hadleigh. Take the A1071 Hadleigh to Sudbury road which bypasses the village.

Follow the signs to Boxford.

Parking: There are several parking spaces in Broad Street opposite the Fleece. In addition,

vehicles park at the kerbside in several streets.

Map: OS Landranger 155 Bury St Edmunds (GR 962405).

Boxford in the 1500s was known for the making of woollen cloth. That trade made it a wealthy place, as can be seen by the many delightful old houses in the village and its fine church.

Wander along Swan Street, passing Weavers House, Old Castle House and next to it Victoria Cottage. At No 35 is a

house called Jacob's, with an inscription saying 'Jacob's Tenements were here in the year of our Lord 1454'. Near the edge of the village you will see what were, till 1969, the single-storey Edwardstone Almshouses (built 1855).

At the junction where Swan Street meets Broad Street the wide-fronted, ochre-washed Boxford Stores has all the hood mouldings picked out in white, which with its grey slate roof makes a charming sight.

This walk takes you north through rich farmland to the small village of Edwardstone. From the church the walk is mainly along field paths through this green valley to the edge of Groton, and thence beside a small stream and later along Butcher's Lane, back to Boxford. In narrow Butcher's Lane you will find a magnificent row of timber-framed black and white cottages with, typically, the upper storey oversailing the ground floor.

THE WALK

❶ From Broad Street, by the Fleece, walk towards the church and almost immediately go right along Swan Street with its fine attractive row of houses. At the end of the village, after passing Daking Avenue on the left, go left on a road signed to Edwardstone. In about ½ mile pass The Winthrops, a road on the left.

❷ At a footpath sign on the far side of Edwardstone Lodge go left through the garden of a dwelling and continue on a waymarked headland path. Where the

hedge ends go straight ahead on a cross-field path to a gap in a thick hedge. Go straight ahead, across the next field. At the far side turn right beside a hedge. Where the hedge makes a bend to the left, go straight on towards the right-hand end of Cowper's Wood.

❸ Cross a sleeper bridge at the corner of the wood and, having followed the wood on the left, cross another bridge at a corner and turn right, on a grassy cart track, with a hedge on the right for 150 yards.

At the field boundary go through a gap, and leaving the cart track keep straight ahead on a narrow path through a newly planted wood. On reaching a large mature oak, go on a few yards and turn left beside a hedge on the right. In about 150 yards come to a gap in the hedge, just before a very old oak tree. Go right, between the tree and a cross-hedge, and cross diagonally a rough uncultivated field, passing another great tree.

The path leads out to a gravel drive. Go straight on to pass white-painted Home Farm and Edwardstone church on the left.

The magnificent timber-framed cottages in Butcher's Lane.

❹ Having passed the church, leave the track, which swings right, to go straight ahead through a kissing-gate into a large pasture. Swing right and cross this field to a stile at a low point on the right. Cross a narrow plantation, through a gate out to a road.

Cross the road and take a narrow path diagonally through a plantation of young trees. At a corner of the plantation, climb a bank close to an electricity pole and then bear left on a headland path with a hedge on the left, following overhead electricity wires. At the field corner go right about 15 yards, left through a hedge, and continue beside a hedge on the left.

❺ At the end of the field, drop down, crossing a cart track and continue in the same direction over a field towards a broad gap in the far hedge. Enter the next field and follow the hedge on the left as it bends right and left. Eventually, on reaching the corner of the field, beyond which you can see the roofs of some houses, go left through the hedge, over a bridge and turn right. At a field corner go straight ahead, with a cupressus hedge on the right, at the edge of the garden of a bungalow. Pass round an oil tank to a road.

❻ Go right for 10 yards and then, within sight of the White Horse public house, go left, following a grassy path with a ditch on the left. At the corner of the field, cross straight over a sleeper bridge and then continue with the wood on the right. Drop down to cross a sleeper bridge and immediately turn right, still beside the wood.

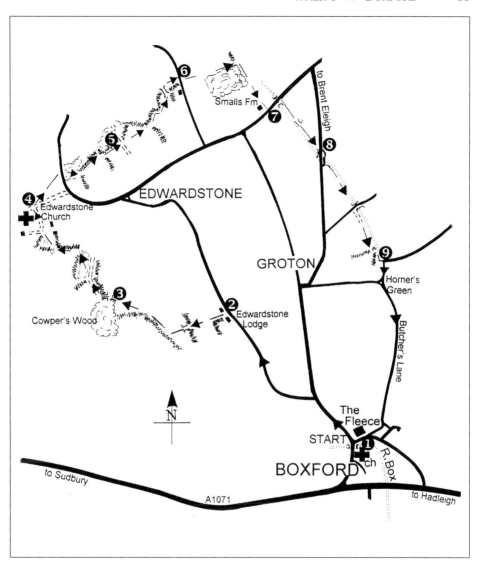

Go left, following a waymark at the south-east corner of the wood, making for the left end of a large house, Smalls Farm. At the far side of the field go half-left on the headland and, passing a pond on the right, go out over a sleeper bridge to the road.

❼ At the road turn left. Walk down to a culvert with short white railings where a ditch crosses the road. Turn right beside the ditch on the right. Cross a substantial plank bridge and continuing beside the ditch, eventually reach a road.

8 Go left a few yards and then loop round to the right on a hard gravel track. In a few yards go left on a grassy path beside the stream on the left. In 300 yards cross a road to walk along a gravel track which soon becomes a narrower path. At the field boundary drop down and swing left immediately to go through a zigzag fence into a hazel thicket where the path swings right. After a gradual turn to the left reach a road at a bend.

9 Turn right along a narrow lightly trafficked road. On reaching Horner's Green, a road junction at a grassy triangle with an ornamental tree, bear left along Butcher's Lane. In ½ mile the road bears left into a housing estate. Turn right before the houses and continue along narrow Butcher's Lane. Very soon, after passing a terrace of old dwellings, return to the start of the walk.

NAYLAND

Length: 6½ miles (or 6 miles)

Getting there: The village is just off the A134 Sudbury to Colchester road.	Parking: There is a small parking bay just beyond the Anchor, and limited parking in the High Street.	Maps: OS Landranger 155 Bury St Edmunds and a very little on Landranger 168 Colchester (GR 974340).

The lovely village of Nayland lies by the river Stour on Suffolk's border with Essex. This is Constable Country and in St James's church is a painting by John Constable of *Christ Blessing the Elements*, which he painted in 1809.

Take time to look at Court Knoll, a moated five-acre raised open area which is believed to be the original site of Nayland.

It is now an ancient monument. During the Middle Ages a manor house stood on the Knoll.

In High Street, where the road widens out, see on the corner extensive, rambling Alston Court. This timber-framed Grade I listed building dating from the early 16th century was once the home of a wealthy clothier. Nearby is the tall somewhat unusual milepost. Wander down Fen Street, too, where a stream separates the attractive cottages from the road, each house having its own little bridge.

There are many delights on this lovely walk, which takes you along the tree-lined river Stour and pleasant grassy paths to Wiston, with its mill and church. Through wonderful leafy countryside, the walk returns to Nayland past the Horse Watering where, a notice explains, horses and other stock have been watered for centuries on their way to and from market at Colchester and Sudbury.

THE WALK

❶ Start by the Anchor Inn, and go a few yards along the road to the bridge over the river Stour. Cross the road and take the footpath signed 'Stour Valley Way', down some steps, and walk beside the Stour on your right. At the weir follow the river bank round to the left and eventually climb an embankment up to the main road. Turn right beside it, walking across a grass sward.

❷ At the crossroads, Nag's Corner, go left on the road signed Wissington, but 20 yards from the junction go left over a stile, into a meadow. Keep to the edge of the field, and later, beside a small stream on the left. Cross a stile at the field corner, and continue in the direction shown by a waymark to a timber bridge and another stile.

Continue along the next field, a ditch on the left, and at the field boundary go right for 15 yards and then left across a timber bridge to continue on a grassy path, with a slight ditch and hedge on the left. To the right, at the top of the hill, is an airfield. The name 'Nayland' appears as a mown strip on the hillside. Immediately before reaching some barns on the left, look out for a waymark indicating a footpath going left. Take a short 200 yard detour along this path for an attractive view of Wiston Mill, then return to the original path.

Continuing the walk, keep on the broad grassy path beside a hedge on the left. Cross the access path to Wiston Mill and go straight on. Pass through a field boundary and continue as before, soon with the tree-lined river Stour on the left. Amongst the trees ahead is Wiston church.

Where the Stour Valley Way goes left over the river, leave it and continue straight on, bearing slightly right, away from the river. Shortly there will be a moat to the right of the path. Keep beside the moat as it bears round to the right, then the brick wall of Wiston Hall is on the left. Turn right at a footpath sign, and then following a waymark go left beside a fence on the right, to the church of St Mary the Virgin at Wiston.

Wiston church.

For the short cut, if you turn right along the drive and walk ½ mile to the road, you can cut off a corner, rejoining the walk at ❺.

❸ Cross the churchyard, passing the south porch, and out at a gate on the west side. Keep on a pleasant grassy path, still following a stream. Look out for a number of very mature willow trees. A little later there is a plantation on the right, at the end of which cross two stiles in close proximity, then cross a pasture to another stile. Turn right up a cart track, go out to the road and turn right.

❹ Walk along the road for nearly ½ mile and follow it round a sharp bend to the left, where a minor road from Wiston

church comes in on the right. Some 200 yards further on the road bends sharply right, but here go left up Campions Hill.

❺ In about 50 yards go left, off the road, at a footpath sign and continue with a field boundary on the left. Soon, in a deep ditch on the left, is a stream. On the hill ahead, the former Jane Walker Hospital can be seen. At the field end keep beside the stream on the left. Cross the stream by a

---

PLACES of INTEREST

East Anglian Railway Museum, Chappel Station.
Open every day except Christmas Day. There are roughly 30 'steam days' a year. Telephone: 01206 242524.

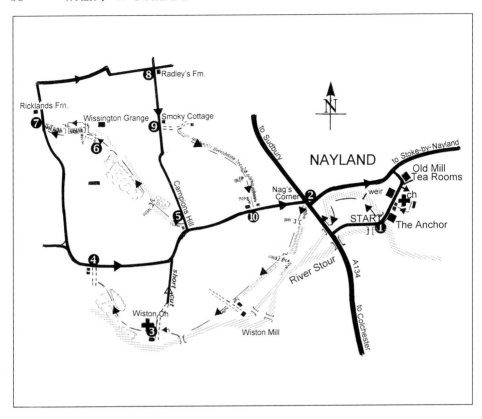

small culvert and pass a pond on the left. Continue on a grassy path with the stream on your right. The pleasant grassy path up a shallow valley has a young plantation on the left and a thick hedge on the right. Eventually the path narrows beside another pond on the left. Rest, if you will, on a seat on the right.

Just beyond the pond cross a stile and then bear half-left, climbing up to another stile at the corner of a fenced field. Go right, following the fence on the right and then at the end of the field cross a stile. Wissington Grange is over to the right.

❻ Go on a wide grassy path through a small glade containing a variety of trees, the stream is still on the right. At the end of this ornamental wood go right, over the stream and cross a stile at the top of a bank. Immediately turn left, keeping a fence on the left. At the corner of the pasture, go left over a stile and descend a few steps, cross a ditch and climb steps the other side. Turn right and continue on a broad, well-walked grassy headland beside a ditch on the right. At the field corner cross a bridge out to a road and turn right.

❼ Walk along this little-used road for ¼ mile. At the road junction go right towards Leavenheath along a narrow country road.

In spring the orchard on the left is an attractive sight. In a little over ¼ mile, the road makes a sharp bend to the right and then goes left. Eventually you come to a crossroads where, at the corner, is Radley's Farm.

❽ Turn right towards Wiston church. In ¼ mile, pass a cream painted house on the right and Smoky Cottage on the left. Immediately after, go left at a footpath sign.

❾ Walk along a broad cart track and in 100 yards, where the track bears slightly left up to a farm, go right at a sign, downhill. Continue in the valley with a small stream and bank on the left. The airfield is at the top of the hill on the right. Keep beside the stream for ¼ mile or more. Eventually come to a cross-hedge where you cross a bridge and stile, and continue

in the same direction through another pasture. Enter a grassy lane by a stile and after two more stiles in quick succession, go out to a road and turn left.

❿ In ¼ mile, reach Nag's Corner on the A134 where you were earlier ❷. Cross straight over and go straight on into the village. Continue along Bear Street, looking out for the Nayland Horse Watering on the right. At a T-junction turn right. Pass the Old Mill Tea Rooms on the left and a little further on, turn left into Church Lane. Turn right, passing the churchyard and the timber-framed White House, and then right again to walk along the passageway beside the south porch of the church, back to the High Street, near Alston Court and the Milepost. Turn left along Court Street, passing the opening to the historic Knoll, back to the Anchor Inn and the start.

RATTLESDEN

Length: 3 miles

Getting there: Rattlesden is 5 miles west of Stowmarket. Follow the A14 and leave it at the junction with the A1088, but take the road south towards Woolpit. Follow the signs for Rattlesden which is about 2 miles away.

Parking: In Lower Road there is a layby opposite the Brewer's Arms and the village hall. In addition there is some parking by the shop, post office and community centre in a high cul-de-sac just off the main road.

Map: OS Landranger 155 Bury St Edmunds (GR 978589).

This attractive village centres round the church on the hill. At one end, up a lane above Whalebone Cottage and the Whalebone Arch, is the school. At the other end, at the corner of High Street, is a pleasant row of cottages with dormer windows and a mansard roof. A short walk up the hill beside the Brewer's Arms passes some old cottages and gives a good view over the village.

St Nicholas's church is richly endowed with carved wooden angels in the roof. The circular staircase in the tower is an elegant feature. Consider, when in the

FOOD and DRINK

The Brewer's Arms is on Lower Road facing up to the church. Meals are served every day except Monday. Such delicious meals and such attractive presentation too. Dishes on offer include breast of chicken with cream tarragon sauce, pan-fried pork with mandarin orange sauce and medallions of fillet steak with a wild mushroom sauce. Bright brass and copper adorn the immaculate bar and dining room. At one end of the dining room is a long bread oven, door open, peels at the ready and illuminated inside. Next to it is a smaller cooking oven. Telephone: 01449 736377.

On the south door, besides the door handle, is a Sanctuary Handle, the grasping of which by a fugitive was thought to keep him safe from arrest.

Above the village, on the south-west side, is Rattlesden Airfield. Nearby is a memorial to the 447th Bomb Group of the USAF 8th Air Force; B-17 Flying Fortress aircraft flew from this base. American airmen who were stationed here during the war return at intervals to meet with their comrades.

The walk, passing the pretty cottages at Birds Green, sets out on field paths through this pleasant landscape of hills and valleys. The Rattlesden river, woodland and farmland form the background as the route includes Clopton Green and passes Clopton Hall before returning to Rattlesden past St Nicholas's church.

church, how anyone would walk from the top of the stairs in the south aisle along the top of the narrow parclose screen to the next set of stairs leading up to the rood loft. Surely one would need a high-wire artiste's balancing pole, or nerves of steel?

St Nicholas's church, Rattlesden.

THE WALK

❶ From the Brewer's Arms go east and where the main road swings left, go straight on along Birds Green, a minor road. At the bend by a triangular green go left-ish, on a track leading to the recreation ground. Go to the right of a brick pumping station and continue along a concrete track. At the end of the concrete road continue on a narrow footpath through a rough uncultivated area, rising slightly.

❷ The path leads out through a gap in a hedge to the corner of a field. Go straight on beside a hedge on the left. At the field corner descend, cross a stile and enter a pasture. The Rattlesden river flows along the left-hand side of this field. Walk straight on with the field boundary on the right. Cross another stile close to a lone oak and continue in the same direction. Go out over a stile to a road at a bend.

❸ Turn left along the road and almost immediately cross the Rattlesden river. In about 50 yards, where the road bends to the left go sharp right along a minor road.

❹ Soon after passing through a small wood, the road makes a sharp bend to the right. Here go left along a wide farm road for ¼ mile to Clopton Hall.

❺ Keep to the track and pass a pond on the left and a large farmhouse and continue with a hedge on the left. The road swings left through an avenue of trees, passing Clopton Green on the right, and out to a road.

PLACES of INTEREST

Woolpit and District Museum, The Street, Woolpit is 2 miles north of Rattlesden, just south of the A14. It depicts the life of a Suffolk village, and is open from April till September on weekends and Bank Holidays from 2.30 pm to 5 pm. During August it is open on Thursday afternoons. Telephone: 01359 240822/240764.

---

❻ Turn left along the road, passing a bungalow on the right. After a bend to the right and a sharp bend to the left you come to Francis Farm, where a pink farmhouse stands well back on the right.

❼ Turn right at a footpath sign, along the drive beside the farm house on your left. Immediately swing left close behind the house and after passing the back door, go straight on through a gap into a garden and then bear slightly right to the corner of the garden. Go through a gap into the farmyard.

Turn left for a few yards and then right beside a large wooden farm shed, keeping a large green tank on the left. At the corner of the building, beside a wooden electricity pole, go straight out to a field. Turn left along the headland for a few yards to the corner of a large field. Take a cross-field path towards a hedge and on reaching it go left and follow the hedge round to the right.

❽ Look out on the left for a wooden electricity pole with three guy lines (supporting wires). On getting to a point where a ditch on the right ends, go left on a cross-field path to the electricity pole. Then turn half-right to the next pole. The

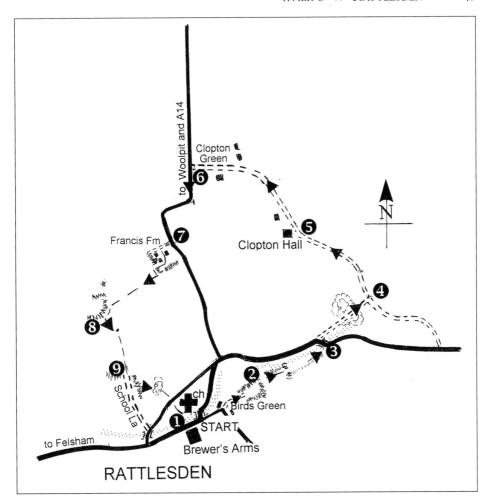

RATTLESDEN

path continues slightly right and leads to a lane at the corner of the field.

9 Go straight on along the lane. In 50 yards go left over a stile, across a garden and through a small pedestrian gate. Then continue on a cross-field path towards the church. Leave the field by a pedestrian gate and go along a path through a small copse. After another gate continue beside a fence on the right, through a large grassy garden. Go out at another pedestrian gate to cross the road and walk down a footpath skirting the churchyard. At the next road go right and continue round to the right, back to the start.

STRATFORD ST MARY

Length: 4½ miles

Getting there: Stratford St Mary is on the Suffolk border, 10 miles from Ipswich. Leave the A12 at the slip road at the northern end of the village and continue through the village.

Parking: The main road through the village is wide and could accommodate some on-street parking. Customer car parking is available at the pubs.

Maps: OS Landranger 155 Bury St Edmunds, 168 Colchester (GR 042343).

Stratford St Mary, bordered on the west by the river Stour, is an important part of Constable Country. East Bergholt, where John grew up, is only 2 miles away and he painted all around this area. On the hill just beyond Stratford is Langham church and vicarage where his wife Maria often stayed, and where he courted her.

Stratford, now bypassed, was on the coaching route from London. The Swan at that time had stabling for 200 horses. Besides the three present pubs there was also the KIng's Arms at the bend in the road, white with a large single-storey bay.

At the northern end of the village are two delightful half-timbered cottages,

FOOD and DRINK

There are three pubs in the village: the Black Horse at the southern end, the Anchor at the northern end and the Swan in the middle. At the Swan, built in 1520, which has a garden with benches and tables on the opposite side of the road alongside the river, you can get such dishes, mostly home-cooked, as chilli con carne, shepherd's pie, lasagne, coq-au-vin and Merrydown pork, followed by a raft of sweets. Telephone: 01206 322164. Teas and light lunches can be obtained at Bridge Cottage at Flatford (National Trust) when this property is open (see Places of Interest).

called the Ancient House and the Priests House, while at the other end of the village is a broad-fronted, timber-framed house with wide windows, called Weavers. The wide windows were necessary to admit the maximum amount of light when this building was indeed used by weavers in the hey-day of the wool trade.

Through beautiful countryside, this walk follows the lovely river Stour towards Dedham and Dedham Lock. Constable walked to school in Dedham every day from East Bergholt and the route takes you over Fen Bridge, which has replaced the footbridge he probably used. The walk then circles back through fields and woodland to Stratford St Mary.

THE WALK

❶ From the centre of the village, near the water treatment building, walk along the road south towards Colchester. Pass the Black Horse on the left and The Weavers, an old half-timbered house, on the right. Further along the road cross two bridges over minor watercourses and keep on to

just before the main bridge over the river Stour, where the route goes left at a kissing gate.

❷ From the gate walk under the main road, the A12. On the far side go through another kissing gate and walk beside the river on the Stour Valley Path. Keep on this riverside path negotiating several similar gates en route, and passing several old pollarded willows. On the opposite bank is a boathouse vaguely reminiscent of a temple.

About 1 mile from the underpass, go left skirting a house, and return to the river bank opposite the former mill buildings which have been converted into dwellings.

❸ Go right over the lock gate at Dedham Lock, passing the former mill, and walk out to the road and turn right. Just 100 yards to the left is Dedham Bridge where, in the season, boats are available for hire.

❹ About 50 yards along the road, at a footpath sign, turn left along the track and

PLACES of INTEREST

At Flatford, about 3 miles away, is **Bridge Cottage** (National Trust). Close by are **Flatford Mill and Lock, Valley Farm and Willy Lott's Cottage**, all associated with John Constable. Bridge Cottage is open at Easter and from the end of May till November at various times (daily in the high season). Telephone: 01206 298260/298865 for details. There is a National Trust shop; teas and light lunches are served. Boats may be hired here. In Dedham is the **Rare Breeds Farm**, with goats, Gloucester Old Spot pigs, longhorn cows and more. It is open daily from March to the end of September, from 10.30 am to 5.30 pm. Telephone: 01206 323111.

The Ancient House and the Priests House.

then take a narrow path beside a ford. Leave the track at another footpath sign, bearing right along a narrow footpath with a hedge on the right. Pass the entrance to the Rare Breeds Farm. Go straight ahead over a stile, through a small paddock and continue between fences. Cross a stile and turn right along a tarmac drive to a road at a bend at the edge of Dedham village. Do not join the road but immediately turn left, beside Muniment House, and in 10 yards go left over a stile and walk down a farm drive.

❺ Where the hard track goes left to the farm, go half-right and in 100 yards enter National Trust land. You will negotiate several kissing gates in the next ¾ mile. Follow the sign to 'Flatford via river 1¼', taking a path between newly planted hedges

which eventually leads across a meadow towards a large tree beside the river.

❻ Go over a footbridge and follow the river Stour on the left. Keep beside the river until you reach Fen Bridge. This modern footbridge, constructed in 1985, was lifted into place by an RAF Chinook helicopter.

❼ Having crossed Fen Bridge, follow Fen Lane for 300 yards. Go over a backwater of the Stour on a substantial cart bridge, and follow the lane round to the left.

❽ Where the lane turns right beside a white bungalow, go left over a stile beside a small wood on the right. At the end of the wood go over a stile on the right and

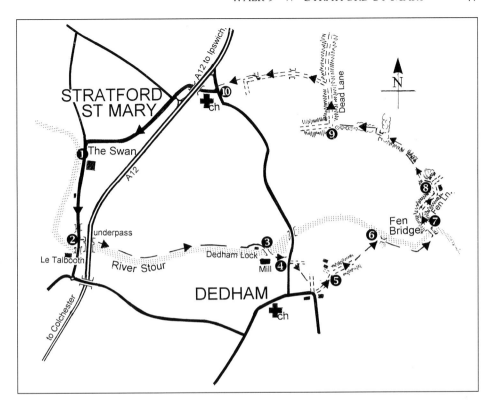

continue beside a fence on the left. At the end of the field cross another stile and follow a hedge on the right for about 100 yards. Go right at another stile and continue, now with a hedge on the left.

Cross another stile in the corner of the field and pass through a narrow shelter belt. Ignore a stile on the left but go straight on over a sleeper bridge and another stile into a narrow field. Turn right for about 50 yards and at the waymark go left through a belt of trees. Soon come out to a headland path with trees on the left.

❾ Eventually, on reaching a three-way junction, go right along a green lane known as Dead Lane. Climbing a little, in 250 yards pass a footpath off to the right, and then go left on a farm track with a hedge on the left. The path gradually bears round towards the church. Cross a culvert at the valley bottom. In a little over 200 yards and shortly before the farm track bends left, turn right over a sleeper bridge. Then turn left, at first beside the ditch and then straight across the field to a road.

❿ Go left for 50 yards along the road and then turn right, passing the church and continue under the A12. Keep on the road through the village, back to your start.

MENDLESHAM

Length: 5 miles (or 4½ miles)

Getting there: Mendlesham is a mile west of the A140 Ipswich to Norwich road. Take a turning to the west, 1 mile north of the 1,000 foot tall TV mast beside the A140.	Parking: There are a few parking places in Front Street just north of the church, and one or two kerbside places in Church Street opposite the church. There are also some spaces in	Old Market Street. Map: OS Landranger 155 Bury St Edmunds, (GR 105658).

Take time to explore the attractive and historic village of Mendlesham. Wander around the oblong of streets, with the church at one end and the Fleece at the other. Weald House is only one of many timber-framed houses in the village.

In Old Market Street, on a small green,

is an enormous stone, an erratic, probably swept here during the Ice Age. It is said to have been used as a Preaching Stone, stood on by Wesleyan preachers when addressing the assembled villagers.

See the patterns in the roof pantiles on the cottage next to the Fleece. At the Old Fire Station on the opposite corner, they

FOOD and DRINK

The Fleece, where Front Street meets Mill Street, is a very old pub. It existed before 1500. In one part of the pub there is an ancient cooking stove, with a bread oven beside it. On a corner is an old built-in washing copper, which would have been used in the days before washing machines were invented. Generous portions of steak and kidney pie, chicken and ham pie, cod, plaice, leek, cheese and horseradish bake, vegan exotic fruit and vegetable curry, and more are on offer. No meals are served on Sunday evening. Telephone: 01449 766511. At the other end of the village in Old Market Street, nearer the church, is the King's Head. A fish and chip shop at one corner of the village seems to do a roaring trade.

have hanging baskets which are old red fire buckets.

Mendlesham is not a large village, yet between 1547 and 1557 no less than seven local people were burned for their religious convictions. It seems unbelievable now as one walks around this peaceful village, but these terrible incidents feature in the village sign.

From the village the walk takes you out to the little settlement of Tan Office where Quakers, unwelcome in the village, long ago founded a tannery. Here you join the route of the Mid Suffolk Footpath for a long time, passing by the source of the river Gipping. Along leafy lanes and through quiet meadows, the walk brings you back to Mendlesham.

THE WALK

❶ From the church go south along Church Road and in 200 yards, where the main road goes left, go straight ahead along a narrow road.

❷ In just over ½ mile, where the road goes sharp right, bear left and immediately right along a narrow surfaced lane, passing Mendlesham House on the left. This tarmac lane ends at the entrance to Ashes Farm on the right. Continue straight on for almost ½ mile along a farm track, to reach the tiny settlement of Tan Office. Many, many years ago Quakers, because of their beliefs, were ostracized and not allowed to live in the village, so they set up a tanning business out here. Pass a white-painted house on the right, which was originally the tannery.

❸ In about 50 yards, turn right at a footpath signpost bearing a waymark for the Mid Suffolk Footpath, a 20 mile route from Hoxne to Stowmarket. Walk along a narrow tree-lined lane then enter a garden, which is the site of the former Quaker burial ground. Keep straight on and at the corner of the garden go through a hedge, turning right at the waymark, beside a hedge and ditch on the right.

In 50 yards or so follow the ditch round to the left on a broad headland track for about 300 yards. Underneath the grid wires, continue in the same direction but now beside a ditch on the left. This is the source of the river Gipping, flowing through Stowmarket to the river Orwell at Ipswich and so out to sea.

❹ At the field boundary cross a culvert into another field and here go half-left towards a yellow waymark in the opposite corner. Some people follow the hedge on the left round to the corner.

Cross a wide culvert and continue on over the next field with a ditch on the left.

The Preachers Stone in Old Market Street, Mendlesham.

About 100 yards or so before the field corner go left over a sleeper bridge and then continue with a ditch on the right. On reaching a corner, follow the boundary fence of some houses left and then right. Cross a ditch, squeeze to the right and go out along a tarmac drive and, at the road, go right for 100 yards to a footpath sign.

For a short cut, continue straight on along the road for ½ mile to Kersey's Cottages ❼.

❺ For the full walk, go left at the sign and then straight across the field. At the far side cross a track, and then some rough grass to a hedge. Turn left at a footpath sign and continue with the hedge on the left. At a corner of the field go right, passing a children's playground on the left.

Go left at the next corner, striding a shallow ditch, and swing round to the right across a cart bridge into a meadow. Go half-left, making for a gate which leads onto a road.

❻ Having reached the gate do not go out to the road but make a U-turn back through the middle of the meadow, following a little-used cart way. Pass close

---

PLACES of INTEREST

Two miles away to the north-west is **Cotton Mechanical Music Museum**, a veritable Aladdin's cave of musical treasures. Open on Sunday afternoon from June through to September. Ample car parking. Light refreshments are available. Telephone: 01449 613876.

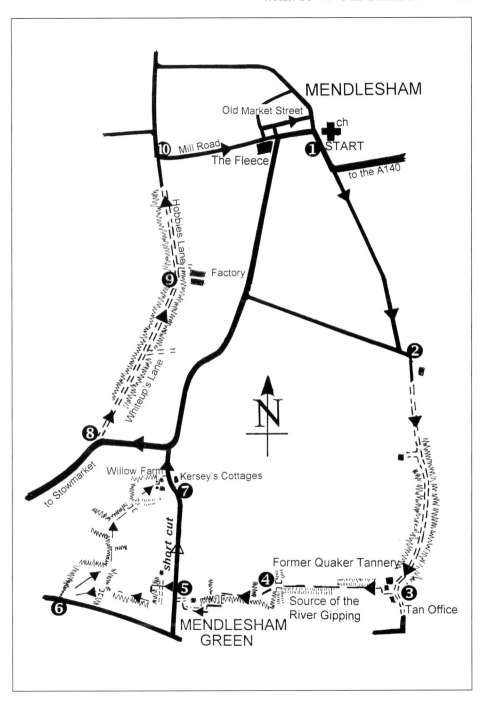

to a field corner and then keep beside the hedge on the left. Go through a cross-hedge and continue with a hedge on the left. Where the hedge turns left, keep straight on across the field, reaching an internal corner by a small pond. Turn right. At the next corner cross a plank bridge and about 10 yards further on, go left over a ditch into the corner of a field.

Make your way towards the middle of the farm buildings on the right. Walk along a broad grass strip between sheds and then in a few yards turn left beside an old corrugated iron Nissen hut, with characteristic circular walls and roof, on the right. Skirt round to the end of the building and cross a stile into some rough uncultivated land. Follow a narrow footpath which soon skirts a fenced paddock. Go over a stile to a road opposite Kersey's Cottages.

❼ Turn left along the road and in 200 yards, at a junction, go left towards Gipping.

❽ In 300 yards, when the road bends to the left, go right on a broad grassy track known as Whiteup's Lane. Shortly after the end of the first field the track is a green lane with hedges both sides. A lane goes off to the right but keep straight on. You pass, behind the hedge on the right, the silos and industrial buildings which form the Mendlesham Maltings.

❾ After a path leads off to the right, the leafy lane ends and the walk continues straight on, now with a ditch on the right and a hedge on the left. Before long, by a house on the right, the lane is surfaced and is called Hobbies Lane.

❿ At the road junction turn right, along Mill Road. Entering Mendlesham, take the first turning left, along Old Market Street, and then bear round to the right. Just beyond the village sign on the right is the old Preaching Stone or erratic. At the end of the Old Market Street turn right, back to the church.

PALGRAVE

Length: 6½ miles

Getting there: Palgrave is just south of Diss and is now bypassed by the A143 Bury St Edmunds to Lowestoft road. Follow the A143 and take the turning to Palgrave, 1 mile east of Wortham.

Parking: There is no convenient parking which can be recommended in the village, so the walk starts at a parking place on the edge of a common, Wortham Ling. From the church, go north to descend Denmark Hill towards Denmark Bridge and Diss. Take the second turning to the left (½ mile from the church). The car park is 1 mile further, on the left.

Map: OS Landranger 144 Thetford (GR Palgrave church 115784: Wortham Ling 097793).

Palgrave lies in the wide but shallow Upper Waveney Valley on the border of Suffolk and Norfolk. The green, with its many trees, runs through the centre of Palgrave and creates a beautiful setting for a pair of flint-faced houses set off with red lattice-work porches and a variety of other interesting houses. A timber-framed house faces the church across another small green by the village sign. The local ducks have adopted the green. Both the school and the 14th century church are central to the village.

FOOD and DRINK

At Wortham, about 2 miles to the west of Palgrave on the A143, is the Olde Tea Shoppe (look out for the Teapot sign by the roadside). For coffee, teas and home-made meals this fully licensed café can be recommended. On the menu are home-made steak and kidney pie, cottage pie (meat or vegetarian), pasties, ham, egg and chips, treacle tart, cream teas and much more. Open all year round. Telephone: 01376 783210.

Wortham Ling, at the start of the walk, is a large expanse of common where the vegetation is typically sandy heathland. It is a Site of Special Scientific Interest and a Nature Reserve, with plenty to interest the walker. From here you follow the walk into picturesque Palgrave village, and then take an easy route west to Wortham – where you can take a break at the Olde Tea Shoppe! Return through peaceful country-side to Wortham Ling Common.

THE WALK

❶ From the parking area at Wortham Ling, go along the road towards Diss and Palgrave. In nearly ¾ mile, at a footpath sign turn right along a grass path. Go through a field boundary and continue beside a young hedge on the left. Keep straight on at a footpath sign, now beside a ditch on the left.

❷ Turn left along a narrow road, and after passing the parish cemetery turn right at a T-junction and enter the village. Look out for a pond on the right and Malt House

A fine timber-framed house stands on the green opposite the church.

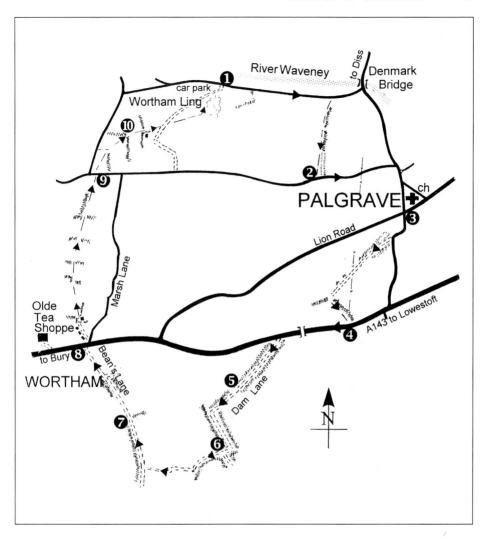

opposite. Walk along the green, bearing right, to pass the church on the left.

❸ Cross straight over Lion Road and follow Priory Road towards Thrandeston. The road bends right, and further on makes a sharp bend to the left. Here following a footpath sign, go straight on along a hedge-lined lane. Before long the hedges give way

to open fields on both sides. After about 200 yards go underneath grid lines and in another 200 yards, the lane ends at the entrance to a field. Go left over a stile and then follow the hedge on the left, eventually crossing a stile to a road.

❹ Cross the road and turn right along the verge for ¼ mile. About 50 yards beyond a

PLACES of INTEREST

Bressingham Steam Museum and Gardens are just 2½ miles west of Palgrave. There are several narrow gauge railways you may ride on, steam traction engines, fire engines and many historic steam locomotives to see. There is a restaurant and a shop. Telephone: 01379 687386. Adjacent to the Steam Museum is the **Bressingham Plant Centre**. The open season is from April through to November. Telephone: 01379 687382.

farm bridge, tun left along a narrow hard track called Dam Lane.

❺ In a little under ½ mile the hard surface ends. Continue straight ahead on Dam Lane which is now a leafy footpath which, after 300 yards, makes a sharp turn to the left. In ¼ mile come to another corner, this time to the right and, 100 yards beyond, leave Dam Lane which turns sharp left.

❻ Keep straight on along a well-used track with a hedge on the left. In 300 yards bend right and continue along the cart track. On reaching a hedge and a junction of tracks, turn right beside the hedge on the left.

❼ Come to a cross-hedge and keep straight on along Bean's Lane. Before long the lane passes a stand of mature trees and then continues out to the A143 road at the edge of Wortham. The Olde Tea Shoppe is about 300 yards away to the left.

❽ Crossing the road, go down Marsh Lane. In 10 yards swing left at a footpath sign, along a gravel track with several houses on the left. At the end go straight

on through a gate into the garden of North Cottage. Pass the end of the cottage and at the corner of the garden stride a narrow ditch and reach the corner of a field.

Go north on a cross-field path. On the far side go over a culvert into a field. Continue with a hedge on the left at first, but in 10 yards take a cross-field path in the same direction. Later cross a sleeper bridge attributed to the Upper Waveney Valley Project. Keep in the same direction across two more fields. At the next field continue beside a hedge on the left, and then along a broad lane.

❾ Come out to a minor road, cross a stile in the hedge opposite and go half-right as waymarked, towards a large oak. Go through a gate to cross another field diagonally to a stile. Cross the next field making for a point about 50 yards to the left of the white farmhouse.

❿ Come out at a gap in the hedge beside the garden of the farm and walk straight on, over some rough ground, to the common known as Wortham Ling. Bear left across the common, back to the car park and the start.

PIN MILL

Length: 5 miles (or two circular walks of 2 miles and 3 miles)

Getting there: Pin Mill, a part of Chelmondiston, is 6 miles from Ipswich on the western bank of the river Orwell. Take the B1456 towards Shotley, turn left in	Chelmondiston for Pin Mill. **Parking:** There is a pay-and-display car park in the village. On the track beside the shore	there are public conveniences. **Map:** OS Landranger 169 Ipswich (GR 205379).

Pin Mill is a small picturesque hamlet on the western shore of the river Orwell. It lies in a sheltered bay where the river changes course, and not far from the end of the Shotley peninsula, that tongue of land which lies between the rivers Stour and Orwell.

From Shotley Point up to Ipswich

docks is about 10 miles, and quite large boats still go up to discharge their cargo. The wide stretch of water of the Orwell Estuary makes it ideal for sailing and Pin Mill is one of several boating centres along the river. Many of the craft which sail these waters are moored just off the shore. At Regatta times the mast at the sailing club is resplendent with colourful flags. Arthur Ransome, of *Swallows and Amazons* fame, based his book *We Never Meant To Go To Sea* on Pin Mill.

On the opposite shore to Pin Mill can be seen Orwell Park House, in Nacton, built in 1770 and now a prep school.

The walk passes through Cliff Plantation, 17 acres of cliff-top woodland bought by the National Trust in 1979 with money given by Mrs Maud Rouse in memory of her husband Philip who died in 1966. The Great Storm of October 1987 devastated the woodland but the Trust planted 43,000 tiny saplings to make good the damage.

This fascinating walk, with so much to see, takes you out of the village past St Andrew's church, and up onto the tree-clad slopes of the estuary. Pause a while to enjoy the wonderful views of the river before continuing past the Sailing Club and along riverside paths. Splendid Woolverstone Hall and church are passed on the return, as well as Cat House with its smuggling connections.

THE WALK

❶ From the car park access way, go through the picnic area to a stile at the far corner. Twenty yards beyond go over another stile into a large field. Climb diagonally up this field. At the top leave by a stile, to join a hard farm track which in 250 yards comes to a road at a T-junction. Turn left, passing St Andrew's church and very soon bend left and then right and walk down the winding road, eventually passing Wendy Close and reaching the Pin Mill road by a grassy triangle.

❷ Cross straight over and climb a gravelly track with hedges both sides which snakes right then left, to meet a farm track by several barns. Go straight ahead swinging round the end of the barns, along a sandy grassy-middled lane. In ½ mile, at the corner of a wood, enter a tree-lined curving track which descends to a small lake. On the left are many young sweet chestnut trees.

Go over the stile beside a farm gate, bearing the legend 'Clamp House Footpath Only'. The paths at Clamp House may be altered in the future, but unless the waymarks indicate differently, cross the

PLACES of INTEREST

Alton Water, 3 miles away, is a man-made lake about 3 miles long where many water sporting activities take place and where there are nature reserves. It is just off the B1080 road at Stutton. There is a visitor centre and tea rooms. Telephone: 01473 328628. At Shotley Marina the **HMS Ganges Association Museum** portrays the HMS Ganges Boy's Training Establishment from 1905 till 1976. It is open from April till October on weekends and Bank Holidays from 11 am to 5 pm. Telephone: 01473 684749/787291.

stile and continue along the track through the trees. The track goes towards Clamp House passing a deep pond on the left.

❸ Just beside Clamp House go left, passing a weatherboarded barn with red pantiles on the right. Go straight ahead into a narrow path that climbs up through woodland of the National Trust's Pin Mill Cliff Plantation. The path continues for ¾ mile through the woods near the edge of the steep bank down to the shore line on the right. There are two places to relax on a seat beside the path, and to enjoy the excellent views of the river. Nearing the village, the wood gives way to a field on the left and the sandy path swings left skirting some gardens.

❹ In a few yards, turn downhill, cross the head of a cul-de-sac and descend steps to the road. At the bottom turn right and pass the entrance to the car park. This is the completion of the 2 mile walk.

Continue downhill to the Butt and Oyster public house. Go left along the shore and very soon leave the river, swinging left, passing the Pin Mill Sailing Club.

❺ Beyond the buildings, turn right at a junction of tracks and continue on a narrow lane beside a yacht compound.

❻ Where the lane goes left, keep straight ahead through a kissing-gate and continue beside a narrow wooded bank, which slopes down to the river. Go almost on to the shore for a few yards at a field boundary, and continue along the well-used path. Eventually go through a gap in a hedge beside an overgrown stile

underneath an ancient oak.

❼ Keep straight on along a cross-field path. Half-left you can see Woolverstone Hall, a Palladian mansion and now home to Ipswich High School. The cross-field path leads into a small wood. At the next hedge, at the footpath sign turn right on a well used path running down towards the shore. Follow the path, which leads through an old kissing-gate beside the Royal Harwich Yacht Club. Keep to the right of the lawns, following the edge of the tideway. Pass beside the signal station to reach a concrete roadway.

❽ Turn left here and pass, behind trees on your right, Cat House. It is said that a china cat was left in the window as a signal to smugglers in days long gone. Keep along the road which loops round Cat House and then has a yacht storage area on both sides. About 20 yards before the end of the concrete storage bays, go left at a footpath sign, down some steps and into the woods.

Soon leave the woods and emerge into parkland. Hug the left edge of the parkland and in about 100 yards at a waymark enter the woods on a narrow path. At the end of the woods come out to playing fields. Keep straight on, as waymarked, and pass 14th century Woolverstone church, with its flint-faced tower, on your left. At the road go left for a few yards.

❾ At a junction opposite the south porch of the church, turn right for 10 yards then go left, over a stile, into a field. Walk parallel to the fence. On the left you can see the tower and stable block of Woolverstone Hall. Cross another stile,

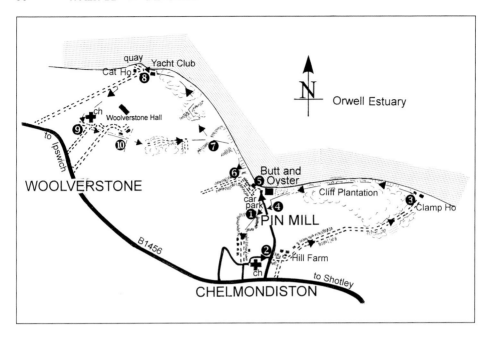

then continue beside a fence on the left.

❿ At a corner of the fence go straight across a cross-field path towards some trees, then follow a grassy path through the wood which swings round to the left. Pass a small pond, and continue beside a wood on the right. After swinging right into the woods for a few yards emerge at the side of a field. Where the cart track goes sharp right, go straight on across the field. At the far side rejoin the path you were on earlier, underneath an old oak tree **❼** and retrace your steps along the path beside the river, back to Pin Mill.

EARL SOHAM

Length: 4 miles

Getting there: Earl Soham lies on the A1120 road between Stowmarket and Yoxford, 13 miles from Stowmarket.	**Parking:** There is a good layby alongside the A1120 main road through the village. Alternatively, cars park under the trees beside the roads	which skirt the green. **Map:** OS Landranger 156 Saxmundham (GR 232631).

Earl Soham has a long history. How many villages have a bowling club founded as early as 1789? The bowling green is, not surprisingly, opposite the Falcon public house. At the western end of the village is a long range of cottages with brick ground floors and red and black half-timbered upper storeys, jettied out on stepped brick

corbels. White doors set off the terrace, which is topped by a pediment and huge chimney stacks. This terrace was, until the early 1800s, a maltings – it adjoins the Victoria pub and its brewery.

Further eastwards is the white-railed bridge beside white Bridge Cottage. On the south wall of that building, facing the

FOOD and DRINK

The Falcon, which is in the centre of the main street, serves meals lunchtimes and evenings, seven days a week. Many of the dishes are home-made. You can choose from steak and kidney pie, ham, egg and chips, beef curry, seafood platter, pork schnitzel and more. Then there is home-made fruit pie and cream, banana split, treacle sponge pudding, spotted dick and ice creams. The Falcon dates back to at least 1540, with a ghost and strange unexplained, strong and very localized smells of TCP on occasion! Telephone: 01728 685263.

trim secluded garden, is a fine sundial.

Moving eastwards you come to a pink house facing a cream-washed thatched cottage which stands next to grey St Mary's church. Slightly behind the church is a fine old house that once was the rectory, white and bay-windowed.

Any walk in this lovely part of Suffolk is a delight and this is no exception. Undulating fields and woods entice you out along grassy paths and well marked tracks, then bring you back to Earl Soham. On the way you have a view of the beautifully restored post windmill at Saxtead Green.

THE WALK
❶ From the green at the south-western end of the village street, walk along the road towards Stowmarket for a few yards. Go right along a narrow path beside the post office. In a few yards cross a narrow cul-de-sac and continue on a narrow path which leads into a corner of a large field.

A relaxing scene in the village.

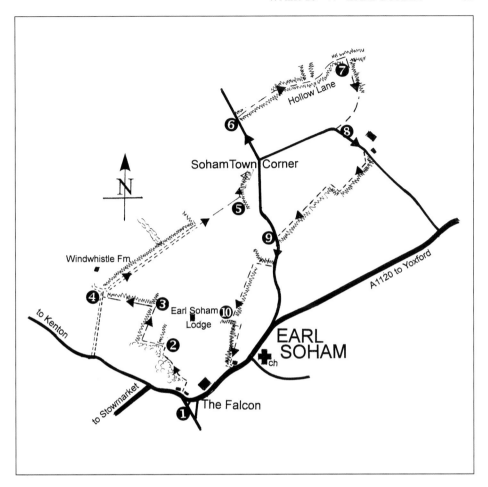

Turn left on a headland path. At a corner turn right and follow the field edge round several bends, with light woodland on the left and the rising field on the right.

❷ The path climbs and in about 100 yards, by two big electricity poles and about 150 yards before a bungalow at the top of the hill, go left over a footbridge. Go straight on, still with rough woodland on the left below you and at a corner turn right, climbing slightly.

❸ As you near the top of the hill turn left with a hawthorn hedge on the right, towards a distant row of poplars. On reaching the field corner, go through the hedge line and turn right along a farm drive beside poplar trees for a few yards towards the farm gate to apricot-washed Windwhistle Farm.

❹ Leave the track and go right for about 20 yards and then swing left on a gravelly track along a crest of a hill for about ¾ mile. Half-way along this path, pass a shelter belt of woodland on the left and a cross-hedge on the right. Keep straight on. In about 200 yards where a hedge on the left ends, keep straight on along a grassy path, to the far side of the field.

❺ Turn left at a footpath sign on a grassy path with a hedge on the right. In a few yards there is a stile in the hedge on the right. The right of way crosses the stile and continues on the opposite side of the hedge. However, local people seem to continue along the headland beside the hedge on the right, which curves round and out to the road at Soham Town Corner. At the road junction go left, walking down the road towards Bedfield and Worlingworth.

❻ At the valley bottom, turn right into Hollow Lane, a bridleway signed to Saxstead Little Green. Follow the lane for ¼ mile. At a junction do not go left along Bullswood Lane, but walk on along the wide bridleway, with hedges both sides.

❼ After some bends, come to a sign pointing through a gap in the hedge. Turn right, following the path beside a tall hedge on your left. Where the hedge ends a grass path continues, swinging right a little across a large open field. Pass a signpost pointing across the field towards Saxtead Green Mill, which can be seen ½ mile away.

On the far side of the field, keeping a hedge on the left, skirt a pond and reach a road at a bend.

❽ Turn left for 200 yards. Just opposite some chicken sheds go right at a bridleway sign, at first with a hedge on the left and a deep ditch. In about 100 yards go right on a path with a hedge on the left. Keep following round the edge of this very large field to reach a road.

❾ Go left along the road and in 200 yards go right and follow a cart track with a hedge on the right. At the corner of the field go left and take a grassy track beside a hedge on the left.

❿ At the corner of the field go left, over a bridge and immediately turn right with a hedge on the right. After a gap in a cross-hedge continue, passing a playing field, and come out beside the school, turn left and then right back to your start.

WALK 14

METFIELD

Length: 5½ miles (or 3½ miles)

Getting there: Metfield is about 6 miles west of Halesworth, on the B1123 Halesworth to Harleston road.	**Parking:** There is a reasonable amount of streetside parking if you choose the wider parts. The Duke William has a large	customers' car park. **Map:** OS Landranger 156 Saxmundham (GR 295803).

Metfield for the most part comprises a quadrangle of interesting roads – from the village shop past the pub to the church, turn left and so on round. Opposite the east end of the church is attractive Street Farm, with the village sign on the green in front. At the bend in the road further north are more colour-washed old houses. Turning south from the green there is a

pleasant assembly of brick houses both sides of the street. See at Rose Cottage the decorative white eaves and the two white medallions, in deep relief, on either side of the gabled porch.

There has been a school house in Metfield since about 1590. One aspect of school life around 1910 is very surprising by today's ideas. The then schoolmaster provided a miniature rifle range. Who used it: the staff, the villagers, surely not the children?

Try to be in the church of St John the Baptist about ten minutes before the hour, when the clock will begin to whirr and click. The mechanism of the church clock can be seen working in the tower at ground level. Amazingly, the clock has been working here since 1629. A timed push-switch enables you to illuminate the mechanism on dull days. There is a pamphlet about the remarkable clock on sale inside the church. And can you spot the Metfield Imp, in the nave high above the chancel arch?

Most of this pleasant 5½ mile walk is along hard farm tracks and a surfaced minor road, though it goes through one small wood and crosses several fields and pastures. On the way you will enjoy views across the Waveney Valley into Norfolk and pass tiny Withersdale church.

THE WALK

❶ Cross the road opposite the church and take a grass path on the left of a white-painted barn which leads straight into a mown grass path between hedges. Where the grass strip bends left, cross a footbridge, then turn left on a headland path. Soon bear right along a road. In 200 yards, turn right along a narrow minor road.

❷ At the junction, bear right along the 'No Through Road'. After passing close to the base of a windmill on the right and then a house, the track becomes a grass path and swings right. In sight of a farm ahead, go left beside a thick hedge on the left for 100 yards. Continue through a narrow path between the hedge and some bushes and then beside a ditch out to a road. Bear left along the road for about 200 yards.

❸ Turn right along a concrete farm track. Pass a car breaker's yard and shortly after, at the junction of tracks, bear right, keeping the wood on the right. Passing the wood, continue along the concrete road with farm buildings on the left and eventually arrive at a road.

❹ Turn right along the road and 200 yards before the house with a white gable, go left over a culvert into a large field. Cross the field towards a prominent ash tree about

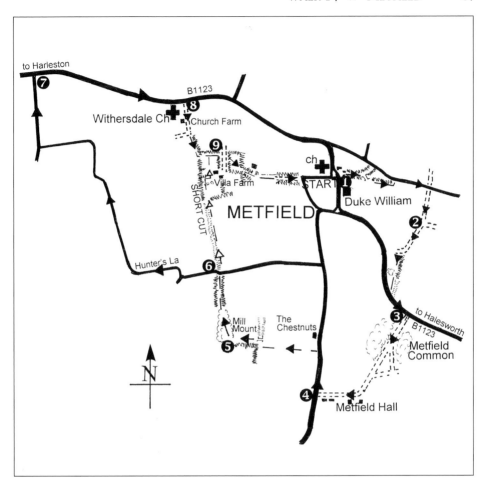

20 yards to the left of a thick hedge, in the background. At the tree, turn right beside a ditch for 20 yards and then go left over a bridge and follow a hedge on the left to the corner of the field.

❺ Cross a stile and enter the woods. About 10 yards into the wood bear round to the right, along a narrow footpath. The path comes out at the opposite corner of the wood, and leads into a narrow grassy lane between hedges. In 200 yards, reach Hunter's Lane.

For a short cut, go straight over Hunter's Lane and, following the sign, walk along beside a ditch on the left. In the corner of the field go over a stile through a thick hedge into a meadow. Walk beside the hedge on the left and after passing a row of bushes, continue to the corner of the field. Turn right beside a thick hedge but soon come to a fence. Turn left through a gate and cross a narrow field to pass through or over a dilapidated gate into another pasture. In the middle of

The churchyard at Metfield.

the field turn right and make for the whitish gate, to rejoin the full walk at ❾.

❻ For the longer walk, turn left along quiet Hunter's Lane for 1½ miles, avoiding two turnings to the left to Grove Farm and Thorpe Hall respectively, and reach a T-junction with the B1123 road from Metfield to Harleston.

❼ Turn right towards Metfield and in just over ½ mile, observe on the right tiny Withersdale church.

❽ Immediately beyond the church go right on a concrete track – pausing to look at the church – and continue straight on, passing Church Farm. Squeeze past a white gate and where the drive bends right go

straight over a stile. At this point you may encounter an electric fence. These are occasionally erected as a temporary measure to contain livestock. The fence should not impede the right of way but if it is obstructing the path, it is quite safe to push it down with a stick and step carefully over.

Carry on to walk beside the hedge on the left. On reaching almost to the corner of the field go left over two stiles in quick succession into a grass field. Cross the paddock to a whitish gate in the far hedge.

❾ Go straight over a farm drive, through a similar gate into another paddock and swing half-right to cross a stile and then a bridge at the opposite hedge. Continue along a narrow path beside a thick-cut hedge and later through a field, following a hedge on the left. At the field corner keep straight on along a grassy lane. You should see Metfield church tower in front. The lane becomes wider and eventually comes out to a road at a sharp bend. Keep straight on and in 300 yards reach the church and the start.

UFFORD

Length: 3½ miles (or 2½ miles)

Getting there: Ufford, now bypassed by the A12 Ipswich to Lowestoft road, lies on the B1438 half-way between Melton and Wickham Market. Leave the B1438 at Ufford and make for Lower Ufford and the village church.

Parking: The roads in the village are mostly narrow but there is room for a few cars at the roadside beside a tall brick wall almost opposite the White Lion, which has its own customers' car park.

Map: OS Landranger 156 Saxmundham (GR 296522).

At the heart of this quiet attractive village in the Deben valley, down a little lane, is the church. It has a most remarkable font cover, 18 feet high and intricately carved. By the church memorial gates are the village stocks.

The many and varied cottages are often painted in delicate pastel shades. White 'Thatched Cottage' on the Melton road has barge boards which appear like ropes, and a white painted, black-studded door. The pale pink bow-fronted post office, the fine gates to Ufford Place, now a small housing estate, and the row of cot-

FOOD and DRINK

The White Lion near the edge of the village, on the road to Bromeswell, serves many home-made dishes such as beef and beer casserole, pork and pepper casserole, lasagne, and chicken in garlic sauce, with home-made steamed puddings or apple pie, hot chocolate fudge cake or toffee and hazelnut pavlova to follow on. The pub serves meals on all days of the week, at lunchtime and in the evening. Telephone: 01394 460770.

tages along by the village sign are some of many visual delights. On the village sign is a horse; it was here that the Suffolk Punch was first bred in 1768. Take time, before or after the walk, to wander around this pleasant village.

This is an easy walk using lightly trafficked minor roads and grassy meadow footpaths. The walk, starting at Lower Ufford, follows the river bank and then crosses Eyke Common to the edge of Eyke, before returning through Bromeswell and across watermeadows to Ufford. Sometimes periods of prolonged rain may make the riverside meadows quite soggy and one would then need sturdy shoes.

THE WALK

❶ Starting at the church, go through the churchyard and leave by a kissing-gate at the north-east corner. Turn right down a grassy area and cross a footbridge over the Byng Brook, then go half-right on a well-used path. After a stile close to the stream, turn left beside a hedge on the left. Cross a footbridge and stile and go half-right to another stile and re-enter the field. Head for the gabled creamy-pink house.

❷ Come out to the road at a stile, turn right along the road until you have passed Tarn House and then, at a stile, turn right through a meadow. Cross the river Deben and turn left along the river bank. Follow the Deben on your left for some way, passing under the railway bridge. If you are over 5' 8" then mind your head! Cut straight across the meadow at right angles to the railway to rejoin the river by some trees. Where the river bends left, cross a stile and walk along the river bank.

❸ Cross a bridge straddling an overflow weir. Here leave the river, going right over a stile on to Eyke Common. Keep alongside the field boundary on the right and soon cross a footbridge over a drainage leat. Head for the middle of the row of houses seen on the hill in the distance in Eyke.

Pass an internal corner of the

PLACES of INTEREST

The Suffolk Horse Museum on Market Hill in Woodbridge is devoted to the Suffolk Punch breed of heavy working horse. The Suffolk Punch originated in Ufford, so a visit here is fitting. The Museum is open from Easter Monday till September, 2 pm to 5 pm. Telephone: 01394 380643. **Easton Farm Park**, near Wickham Market, is 4 miles due north. It is a Victorian model farm. You may watch the cows being milked from a gallery above, see all manner of animals and visit a blacksmith's forge and a food and farming exhibition. There is a licensed tea room. Open March till September, 10.30 am to 6 pm daily except Mondays, and Monday as well on a Bank Holiday or in July and August. Telephone: 01728 746475. **Buttrum's Mill**, a tower mill in Woodbridge, is open from May till September on weekends and Bank Holidays from 2 pm to 6 pm. Telephone: 01473 583352.

The Mill House, Ufford.

Common and go straight on towards a row of trees, aiming for another footbridge. Cross the bridge and continue with a hedge on the left, to leave by a stile beside a gate. The wide green lane leads in 60 yards to the road.

❹ Turn right, climbing for 100 yards, and turn right at a T-junction. In a further 100 yards go right again on this lightly-trafficked road, passing Reeves Hall with its high beech hedge on your right. To your right also are wide views across the Deben valley. At a Y-junction by the barns of Sink Farm bear right climbing a hill.

❺ At the next junction, for a short cut, you may go straight on along Bridge Road back to Ufford. Otherwise turn left

towards Bromeswell.

❻ In about ½ mile, just before the road bends to the right at the '30' sign, go left off the road along a wide farm track towards Bromeswell church on the hill above. Cross an open field and on the far side, with a fence on the right, walk out to a track where three paths meet. Turn right, passing St Edmund's church, and walk down the lane into Bromeswell. At the junction, turn right.

❼ Very soon at the next junction go straight on into Summer Lane. In 200 yards where the road swings right, go left passing Bardwell Cottage. Continue on a track, keeping the cupressus trees on your right. Follow this grassy-middled path as it

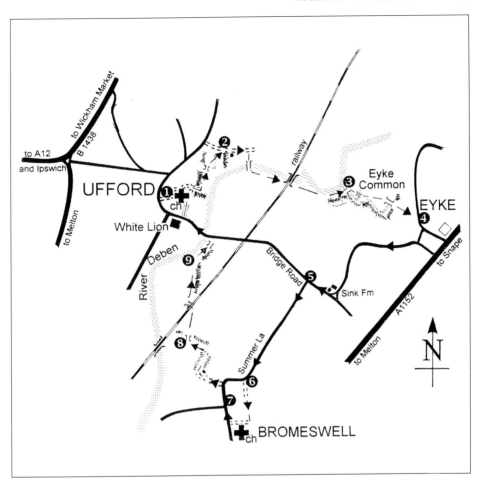

bends right. When the grassy track ends, go left at a signpost and take the path beside a ditch on your right.

❽ About 100 yards before the railway line go right over a footbridge and cross the corner of the field toward a wooden railway stile. Carefully cross the railway line and then a substantial footbridge, descending steps to the field. Look over

towards Ufford. To the right of the church is a row of white cottages with brown tiled roofs. Head for the right of those cottages.

❾ Presently you come once more to the river Deben. Go over a stile and with the river on your left go on to cross a narrow footbridge. Walk out to the road and turn left back to the start.

SHOTTISHAM

Length: From Hollesley Common 7½ miles (from Shottisham 5½ miles)

Getting there: Shottisham is just off the B1083 Melton to Bawdsey road. From a roundabout on the A12, just north of Woodbridge, take the A1152 towards Snape. After crossing the river Deben, at a roundabout, follow the B1083 and in 4 miles turn left to the village. For the start at Hollesley Common: follow the B1083 for about ½ mile and bear left for 2½ miles towards Hollesley, reaching the Picnic Area on the left (ignore Sutton Heath Picnic Area on the right).

Parking: Apart from the yard of the Sorrel Horse, where the landlord may give permission to park, there are few spaces in the village for safe parking. A good place to park, therefore, is the Hollesley Common Picnic Area, where the full walk starts. Anyone parking at the Sorrel Horse should read the walk description starting at point ❹.

Map: OS Landranger 169 Ipswich (GR Shottisham 320446: Hollesley Common 334471).

Shottisham is a small and attractive village set beside a stream which flows down past the former mill to Shottisham Creek. St Margaret's church dominates the village and surrounding countryside, overlooking Church Street with its pretty, often rose-bedecked, cottages. Set in the front garden of a house called Wheelwrights you can

FOOD and DRINK

The Sorrel Horse is a welcoming 14th century smugglers' inn at the road junction near the church. It has a broad range of all home-made dishes, such as rack of ribs in a barbecue sauce, mushroom and celery bolognese with spaghetti, Scotch lamb and herb pie. There are vegetarian dishes in plenty. All the beer is drawn direct from the barrel. Meals are served every day except Tuesday. Twice a year Morris Dancers come to dance outside the pub. Telephone 01394 411617.

still see the steel plate upon which the local wheelwright set the wooden wheels ready to receive the red-hot steel tyres.

This varied circular walk starts across a wide tract of wild sandy heathland to reach Shottisham's quiet village streets. The walk continues over farmland where the soil is very light, relying on irrigation for its success in growing crops. There are fine views towards the estuary at Woodbridge. Half-way round, the walk follows the bank of the river Deben, the haunt of ducks, geese and other wading birds. In summer there is a constant flurry of small craft sailing to the many marinas along the estuary. There is an option to make a shorter circuit starting at the Sorrel Horse.

THE WALK

❶ From Upper Hollesley Common picnic area, walk along the road for 100 yards towards Melton and go left on a sandy track at the first Byway sign. Go through an iron gate and continue on a straight sandy track across fields. In ½ mile cross a sandy track and go straight on along a path through uncultivated heathland.

❷ Cross a track at right-angles and see,

100 yards away on the left, flint-faced 'Stone Cottages'. In another 50 yards at a junction with a sandy track, go half-right. At the corner of a wood leave the cart track, going left on a grassy headland path. In 200 yards where the hedge ends, keep straight on across the field.

❸ At the far side cross another track and go straight on along a well-used, narrower footpath for 120 yards and take the right fork, keeping a wood on the left. Keep to the sandy path beside uncultivated heathland on the left. At a fork go straight on, beside a wood on the right. The lane leads to the end of a surfaced road, here go left into Shottisham along Church Lane, at the end of which reach the Sorrel Horse.

❹ From the Sorrel Horse go right, through the village. In 300 yards at the village sign, go right on a track towards the mill. Go down the mill drive and just before the mill bear left on a gravel drive which leads directly to a stile beside a timber farm gate. There is a fine view of the mill from here. Cross the meadow to a stile, then cross a footbridge and turn right along the road.

❺ In 100 yards go left along the drive towards Wood Hall Hotel. In ¼ mile at the gates to Wood Hall, flanked by two eagles, bear round to the right following the road. Note the expressive Wild Fowl warning sign.

For a shorter walk, missing the path beside the river Deben, keep along the road, to rejoin the main walk at Sutton Hall ❽.

On the main walk, at the Wood Hall

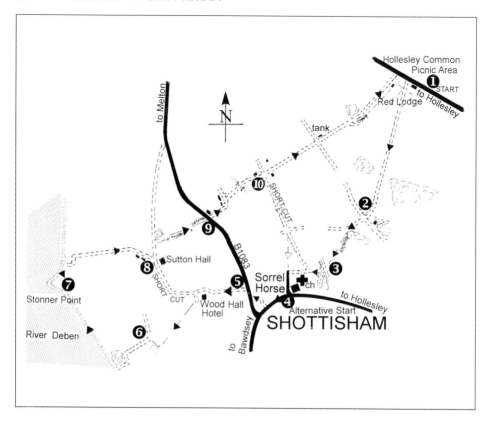

boundary ignore the track to the Coach House and 10 yards beyond it go sharp left on another track, following a footpath sign. Go through the gate to Wood Hall Barn. Just before the barn go right at a waymark through a large metal gate and, passing a brick barn on the left, continue across a pasture to a metal gate on the far side. Cross a track, go right for 10 yards then cross a stile into a field. Continue, first with the field boundary on the left, and then go straight on to a gate.

Continue along a lane between a hedge on the right and, at first, a willow plantation on the left. At the end of the hedge follow the sandy cart track round to the right, passing Rock Hill Wood on the left.

❻ When you come to a junction of tracks at a three-way footpath sign go left along a farm track. The official right of way is parallel to the cart track some 50 yards further along into the field, but the public seems to use the cart track. Ahead there is a fine view of the Deben Estuary stretching away towards Woodbridge. The track skirts the sandy hill on the left, then swings round passing a derelict barn.

On reaching the river Deben, climb the river wall and turn right beside the river. Here there is always something

The Mill at Shottisham.

interesting to see. In the summer, yachts and other craft sail up and down the river. At other times many species of wading birds live in, and around, the shallow waters.

❼ Pass a small promontory called Stonner Point and about 300 yards beyond it, the track swings right, away from the riverside path. Keep to the cart track with grass in the middle. Follow the track round some bends, to a red-roofed barn, and cross a stile beside a gate. Pass through a willow grove, cross another stile and continue with a hedge on the right.

Ignore a little track off to the left, and bear half-right along the main track. Pass a house on the right and in about 200 yards meet a road by a grassy triangle opposite

Sutton Hall, a large brick farmhouse.

❽ Turn left. (Those taking a short cut rejoin the route here.) About 100 yards beyond the farm, reach a small young wood on the right. Here go right on a grassy path and after passing through the wood cross a stile beside a gate and then continue on a headland path for over ¼ mile to a road.

❾ Cross straight over the road and walk along a surfaced byway. Pass several buildings including a thatched bungalow. After a bend to the left, turn right at a three-way junction. There is access here to a Countryside Stewardship meadow. A little further along the byway, cross a bridge with white handrails, and in about 200 yards reach a four-way junction of sandy well-used tracks.

❿ For a short cut and direct return to Shottisham, turn right here. Keep straight on along the sandy track for ½ mile. On reaching a track at Vale Farm, leading to large barns on the left, go straight on for 50 yards. Underneath a large holm oak tree, leave the track and take a narrow footpath half-right across the field. Cross a stile and continue on a narrow footpath which leads out to a lane. Go right to reach Church Lane, and back into Shottisham.

To continue the full walk, go straight on along a very sandy track beside the occasional tree, mostly Scots Pine. Cross another sandy track at right angles, passing a large green tank nearby. The track continues beside fields for ¼ mile and then passes through a gate. Keep on across uncultivated heathland for a further ¼ mile to reach a road. Turn right, back to the start of the walk.

PEASENHALL

Length: 5 miles (or 4 miles)

Getting there: Take the A1120 Yoxford to Stowmarket road. Peasenhall is 3 miles from the A12 at Yoxford.

Parking: There is a small layby on the south side of the main street. There is also kerbside space on the opposite side of the main street.

Map: OS Landranger 156 Saxmundham (GR 357694).

Peasenhall has straddled the Stowmarket to Yoxford road, now the A1120, since Roman times. Not only has Peasenhall an attractive grouping of houses along The Street, its main tree-lined thoroughfare alongside which a deep stream flows, but the village has an interesting history too.

Towards the centre of The Street, next to the post office, is a brick house, Roslyn, with a central doorway and white eaves. Look up to the roof and you will see small lion masks on the guttering. How much more interesting than bland plastic guttering.

In the early 1800s James Smyth and Sons set up an agricultural engineering works here; they invented the Suffolk seed drill. The drill works were up in Church

Street, the hill backing onto the church-yard of St Michael's.

At the start of the walk, as you go towards the east end of the village where the road divides at the Knoll, near the Weavers Tea Rooms, you will see the vil-lage sign. On it is not a painting as on many signs, but a miniature Suffolk seed drill. Round the corner from the Weavers Tea Rooms is a house where a cobbler once lived. His trade sign still projects from the wall.

Just beyond the village sign is a small green, with pine trees and a fine row of old houses facing it, some brick, some half-timbered. The central one was once the ancient New Inn. All now belong to the Landmark Trust, which has carefully restored them.

Leaving the village, the walk continues alongside the river Yox to Sibton and out into the rolling farmland around Peasen-hall. On the road to Sibton White Horse, you also pass the showroom of the wood-turner, Fred Pearson. The river is your companion for the first half of the walk, before turning back towards Peasenhall along peaceful woodland and field paths.

THE WALK

❶ From the main street walk towards Yoxford and fork left at the garage, just by the tranquil green on the right. Further on, glimpse Sibton Abbey away to the left. Turn left along the road to Walpole and soon, after crossing the river Yox, the road runs beside the river.

❷ In about 200 yards go left by the Sibton White Horse, and 100 yards beyond turn left at a footpath sign, cross a foot bridge and continue beside the river on the left. Cross a track leading to a large farmhouse and keep straight on.

After crossing a ditch by a plank, turn left on a cart bridge over the river and then turn right, continuing beside the river on the right. Keep on a wide head-land to the corner of the field, and then keep straight on along a cross-field path. At the far side cross a bridge and turn right along the road.

❸ In about 100 yards cross the river again by some white railings and in a few yards turn left. Do not follow the lane through a gate but keep along a headland path with a hedge on the left. In a little over 100 yards turn left at a 'Circular Route' waymark,

The Knoll, Peasenhall.

crossing a stile beside a gate. This is a permissive path. Walk beside the hedge on the left and at the field corner turn right, walking beside the river Yox. Pass a prominent oak tree about 50 yards away on the right, and still beside the stream, reach at the end of the field a cart bridge on the left and a grassy green lane on the right.

To make a short cut, go left along the cart track up to the road and turn right to rejoin the main walk at Segmore Lane ❼.

❹ The main walk continues through several fields on a farm track beside the river Yox. One hundred yards into the third field, the path moves away from the river slightly, skirting at first a tiny dry pond and very soon a wood on the right.

At the end of the wood cross a culvert

which is the end of the cart track. Keep straight on, along a cross-field path. At the far side of the field cross a ditch at a culvert, about 10 yards from the river bank. Continue beside the river. Soon a hedge starts on the river bank.

❺ On reaching a footbridge, cross the river Yox and continue along its southern bank. (Should the footbridge be missing, continue for a further 100 yards to a cart bridge.) Keep beside the river for about 100 yards and turn left along a good track. Walk up the hill beside a hedge on the left.

❻ Come out on the road between two bungalows and turn left. In 200 yards the road makes a sharp bend to the right, then

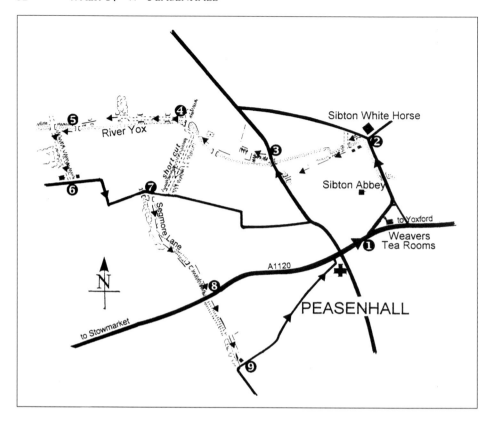

in a similar distance, a bend to the left. In a further 300 yards the road makes a bend half-right and crosses a stream, to pass a narrow belt of woodland on the right.

❼ At the footpath sign, go right over a sleeper bridge along Segmore Lane, a path through the woods. At the top of the hill, where the wood ends, skirt a pond on the left and continue on a good headland path beside a shallow ditch on the left. Half-way along this field from the pond, snake left then right over a two-sleeper bridge, and continue with the ditch now on the right.

❽ At the corner of the field cross a stile, then cross a road and continue beside a ditch on the right. At the top of the slight rise take a narrow path beside a windbreak of poplars. Continue along the path out to a road and turn left.

❾ Follow the narrow leafy road downhill and eventually reach the village church, where the road bends left. Here go right along a lane beside the churchyard wall. At the road turn left back to the village street and the start.

WESTLETON

Length: 6 miles

Getting there: Westleton is 3 miles from the coast on the road (B1125) between Leiston and Blythburgh. From the A12, turn off ½ mile north of Yoxford on a road signed Westleton.

Parking: There is space for a few cars on the road at the southern end of the green fronting the pond, but please do not park on the greens. There is also some street parking in the main street, where the width of the road is suitable.

Map: OS Landranger 156 Saxmundham (GR 441691).

Central to Westleton is a long triangular green, running uphill to its apex. Attractive houses face the green, which is dotted here and there with trees; some of them are memorial trees. At the lower end is a duck-pond with a surprising number of ducks! Several of the village houses have white lattice-work porches, an attractive feature.

Stretching down the Suffolk coastline, roughly between the shore and the A12 main road, is a tract of very light sandy soil called The Sandlings. Here, in times past, the land was wild and uncultivated heath where heather, gorse and birch would grow in profusion. The landscape during the passage of time has been modified.

FOOD and DRINK

The White Horse public house stands close to the village duck pond. You can choose, from a changing menu, such dishes as fresh crab salad, quorn tikka masala, Mexican chilli con carne and chicken curry, followed by tiramisu, apricot crumble and home-made Bakewell tart. Telephone: 01728 648222. The walk passes close to 'Country Teas' at Whimbrel Cottage, on Ride 14. They are open from noon till dusk on weekdays and from 2.30 pm till dusk at weekends. Telephone: 01728 648803.

Forestry is now highly developed over much of the area, and irrigation has enabled cultivation to take place elsewhere, carrots being a frequent crop. In spite of these changes there is still a large area of uncultivated heath in this part of the county, attracting birdwatchers and walkers.

This fascinating walk starts on field-edge paths in the vicinity of the village but soon follows woodland tracks through Dunwich Forest. On the way you pass Potton Hall and the little hamlet of St Helena. Later the path crosses the marshy land beside the Dunwich river, returning through a National Nature Reserve and across open heathland. Bracken and heather bring colour to the landscape during the seasons. The route can be extended to visit ancient Dunwich and the beach, which would add an extra 2 miles to the circular walk.

THE WALK

❶ From the pond at the end of the green, cross the green toward the houses on the left. Half-way up the green turn left at a footpath sign on to a leafy lane. Soon you

are on a broad path which continues straight across the next field. At the far side follow a hedge on the left and go through a cross-hedge, keeping beside the hedge on the left for over 200 yards.

❷ Turn right at a footpath sign, across a field, to pass on the left the end of a cross-hedge. Continue straight on and at a footpath sign go left beside a row of trees on the right. On reaching a cart track, turn right and in about 200 yards cross the Blythburgh road.

❸ Go half-left, (signed 'St Helena 1') on a wide track between fields. Soon you walk beside heathland and a few pines on the right, but later reach a stand of conifers. Here leave the sandy track, continuing straight on along a grassy sward between the pines. Leave the wood and in 20 yards join the farm track to Potton Hall.

❹ Pass the Hall on the right and continue straight on, climbing up a sunken footpath. In a few yards, cross a stile and

PLACES of INTEREST

Dunwich Museum, in St James Street, features a model of Dunwich as it was in the 12th century, and its history over 1,500 years as it lost its battle against the sea. The social history of the area and the wild life is displayed. It is open daily from early April till September, 11.30 am to 4.30 pm. In March it is open weekend afternoons only, while in October it is open daily from noon to 4 pm. Telephone: 01728 648796. **Dunwich Greyfriars** is the site of 13th century monastic remains, open all year round. **Dunwich Heath,** National Trust, is a large area of beach, cliff and heathland, with extensive views. It has a tearoom, shop, exhibition and a lookout. Telephone: 01728 648505.

keep straight on through the forest. After joining a Forestry Cycle Route, keep straight on to reach a road. Turn right and walk for ¼ mile to a crossroads at the hamlet of St Helena.

(For a tea at Country Teas go straight over along Ride No 41, a No Through Road, for about 400 yards. The bungalow is almost opposite Ride No 45. Refreshed, return to the road junction and go towards Dunwich.)

❺ To continue the walk turn right towards Dunwich. Walk down this quiet road. After ¼ mile the road bends half-left by a car park. Continue for another ¼ mile, then leave the road at a footpath sign, going right on a sandy track beside a mature stand of firs on the left. Keep straight on downhill through woods.

❻ At the valley bottom cross two streams and continue through the marsh on a path formed of reeds laid at right angles. Climb away from the marsh and after another bridge cross a stile into a field. Continue with woods on the right. Skirt a farm house on the right. At the end of the field, take a stile out to a lane and turn right (if you want to go into Dunwich you go left here).

In 30 yards, opposite a farmhouse, go left along a stony track. At the road turn right for about 200 yards.

❼ Turn left along a track towards Clay Lane. At the end of the track, go right along a headland path with a hedge on the

The duck pond at Westleton.

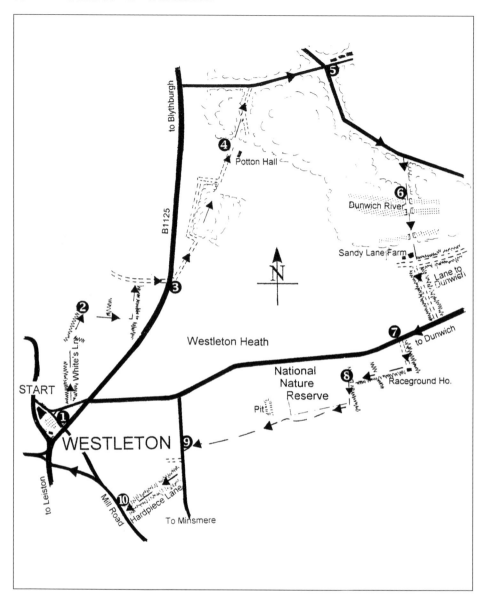

left, through two fields. At the corner of the second field, go left for 3 yards and then cross a stile into the Westleton Heath National Nature Reserve.

❽ The narrow path turns left through bracken, and beside bushes on the left. Soon bend right, the bracken giving way to heather. The path, whilst far from straight, keeps in a generally west-southwesterly direction and eventually leaves the nature reserve at an information board and continues across the Heath. After about ½ mile cross a stile to reach Clay Lane.

❾ Turn left. Pass a track to King's Farm and in another 100 yards turn right on a narrow leafy bridleway with hedges on both sides.

❿ On reaching a narrow road turn right towards Westleton. At the fork in the road, bear left and walk down the hill to the village. Turn right, passing the village hall, back to the start.

Some of the houses in the village have attractive lattice-work porches as shown here.

THORPENESS

Length: 6 miles

Getting there: From the A12 take the A1094 to Aldeburgh, then the beach-side road northwards for 2 miles.	Parking: There is a large pay and display car park close to the shore opposite the Meare.	Map: OS Landranger 156 Saxmundham (GR 472596).

Until 1903 Thorpeness was a small fishing hamlet, called just Thorpe. In 1910 the estate owner, Stuart Ogilvie, built a model village to offer self-catering holidays in an old-world setting with a wide variety of houses. Enjoy a wander round this unique village with its own Country Club, tennis courts and swimming pool, its impressive almshouses facing down the

Whinlands, church and chapel.

Originally water was supplied to the new village from a very functional, but unpleasing looking, metal windpump. Mr Ogilvie brought a windmill from Aldringham and converted it from a corn-grinding mill to a water pump. It was connected to a nearby storage tank on stilts. Later to improve its appearance, the water tank was made into a tall, timber-clad, seven-bedroomed house with the tank still at the top. The whole is affectionately known as 'The House in the Clouds'.

The Meare, a man-made 65 acre shallow boating lake, has canoes and rowing boats for hire. The village founder was a friend of J. M. Barrie, so it was natural that the many islands and inlets in the Meare were given names associated with Peter Pan, which has pleased successive generations of children.

The sandy cliffs which face the North Sea are often eroded when storms lash the coast. In normal conditions the beach, cliff and hinterland of sandy heath form a marvellous area to explore. There is something for everyone on this walk. On the outward route you pass reminders of wartime dangers in the shape of a pillbox and tank traps, with wonderful views out over the sea and the cliffs, while at Sizewell there is the huge white sphere of the nuclear power station (the exhibition centre is open all year 10 am to 4 pm, except Bank Holidays). Turning inland, you come back towards Thorpeness along gorse and heather-bedecked paths, with a closer look at the windmill and the House in the Clouds. The attractive Meare boat-ing lake guides you back finally to the start of your walk.

THE WALK

❶ From the car park walk towards the shore but turn left before the beach, to a road called The Benthills, and climb the road looking out over the sea. At a road junction on the top of the hill, bear right along a road, soon passing the unusual-looking church on the left. At the end of the road, which has become more of a gravel path, go left for a few yards along Admirals Walk and then turn right and in 50 yards follow the road round to the right. At the end, go through a narrow path out to the beach.

Turn left along the shingle to well beyond the last house at the top of the cliffs and a Second World War pillbox perched on the edge. Keep to the foot of the cliffs and soon you will find a sandy grassy path to follow, and a little later you may glimpse ahead the top of the Sizewell Nuclear Generating Station.

Approaching Ness House, on the cliff top, the path gradually climbs and after passing steps down to the right, the narrow path reaches a wide track on the cliff top.

❷ Keep along the top of the cliff. The path runs beside a boundary wall on the left. Later, go straight past several cubical anti-tank blocks, where the path becomes narrower. Pass a derelict gazebo, and continue on top of the cliff. Take the opportunity where you can to look over the cliff at the long beach, often quite deserted. To the left you can usually see fishing boats pulled up on the shore at Sizewell. Later the path drops down and

The Meare, Thorpeness.

cuts under the terracing of Sizewell Hall, a Christian Conference Centre.

Shortly the path runs beside a caravan site. Keep straight on and having passed a house on the left, drop down slightly to the sand-dunes at the foot of the cliffs. Pass the boats and a former coastguard look-out, then go out to the road at the Sizewell Beach car park, which has a café and toilets.

❸   At the road turn left, leaving the beach. Pass the Vulcan Arms opposite the entrance to Sizewell Nuclear Power Station and its Visitors' Centre. Fifty yards beyond a road to Sizewell Hall go right along a farm track. From here you get the first good view of the white sphere of the newer reactor building at the power station.

❹   Just before a house, go left at a bridle-way sign along a grassy track which, in 150 yards, runs beside a wood on the left. Go through a gate at the end of the wood and continue on a cart track, parallel to a fence, about 100 yards away to the right. In over ¼ mile, at another gate, continue through uncultivated heath. Swing round to the left, joining another track, and walk beside a wood on the right.

❺   At the road go left and in a few yards take a tarmac footpath straight on, shortly to continue beside a road. Where the road swings left at a junction, cross the Leiston road and go straight ahead along a broad unsurfaced lane.

❻   At the end of the lane go straight ahead, then swing right a little and left to

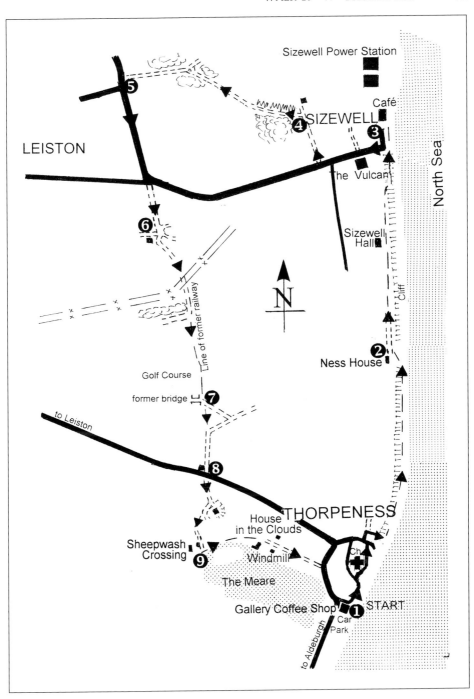

continue on a cart track along the former railway line. You have just passed 50 yards to the right a former railway crossing. Where the cart track goes right, keep straight on along a narrower path, winding through gorse and bracken. Eventually, cross a stile at a path junction and keep straight on, through heathland with the Thorpeness Golf Course on the right.

❼ Go through a kissing-gate, cross a track and keep straight on. In 100 yards join a track coming in on the left and in a further 200 yards, reach a road.

❽ Cross straight over taking a sandy farm track. On reaching a barn in a sand pit bear right and continue on a sandy track. Shortly after, where the track bears left, keep straight on along a narrower grass path. Eventually pass a house, named Mere Cottage 1882, on the right. Just beyond it on the right you will see the remains of Sheepwash Railway Crossing.

❾ DO NOT go to the crossing but turn left along a narrow path, which soon skirts the edge of the golf course with a waterway, part of the Meare, on the right. Soon the path runs up past the golf clubhouse. Continue on a gravel track towards the windmill, which you pass, going between the windmill and the House in the Clouds. The gravel track eventually leads down to the road in the village. Turn right, round past the Meare back to the car park.

SOMERLEYTON

Length: 4 miles

Getting there: Somerleyton is about 5 miles north-west of Lowestoft. Follow the B1074, the village is about 2 miles beyond Blundeston.	Parking: Leaving the village green, on the road marked 'Railway Station 1 mile', you will find some street parking beside the brick wall. At the Duke's	Head, on the walk route, there is plenty of customer parking. Map: OS Landranger 134 Norwich (GR 485973).

Skirted by the river Waveney on its way to the sea, the life of Somerleyton in the late 1800s revolved round Somerleyton Hall, the brickworks, the railway and the river. Sir Morton Peto, who rebuilt the Hall as we know it today and who built the village and the school around the green, was an MP and a great industrial entrepreneur. In 1863 he sold his Somerleyton interests to Sir Francis Crossley, a carpet manufacturer and the great grandfather of the present Lord Somerleyton who lives at the Hall.

The houses around the green are varied and attractive – some thatched, some not, most with dormer windows and

FOOD and DRINK

The Duke's Head, a large and pleasant pub, serves meals everyday, at lunchtime and in the evening. You may have, for instance, steak or gammon, beef and ale pie, chilli con carne or fish. Telephone: 01502 730281.

all with well-kept gardens. There is a quaint thatched, red and white painted school with ornamental chimneys at one end of the green.

In the early days of the Second World War Sir Christopher Cockerell, an engineer who had studied at Cambridge, moved with his family to Somerleyton. It was here in 1958 that he invented the amphibious Hovercraft.

The walk starts by the village green and after skirting Somerleyton Park, crosses farmland to the edge of the river Waveney's flood plain and continues along a path overlooking the river. The route passes close to the old Somerleyton brick-fields, which played a great part in the local economy up to 1939 when the kiln had to be shut down. The glow from its fire which burned day and night for long periods would have been easily seen from the air by enemy aircraft. Skirting a boat-yard by the river, the return route takes you to round-towered Herringfleet church and a magnificent 17th century barn.

THE WALK

❶ Starting from the green, go south-west along the village street beside the Somerleyton estate wall on your left.

The charming and unusual village school at Somerleyton.

❷ In 300 yards, by a wooden First World War memorial seat, turn left along a lane. At the entrance to Glebe House, go straight ahead through a kissing-gate. In a few yards, walk beside the 'Somerleyton' wall for 200 yards to reach the Blundeston road by a chevron sign. Cross the road and turn right along the verge opposite and climb the hill. Pass a metal five-bar gate with, unusually, two latches and keep on to pass the entrance drive to St Mary's church. Cross the road and continue along it for a further 100 yards to a footpath sign.

❸ Leave the road turning right over a stile and beside a hedge on your right, go on to cross another stile and join a sandy track at a bend. Go straight ahead on the green lane which soon bends gradually round to the right. Pass on the left a cottage and an old black weatherboarded, thatched barn. Wicker Well was once a large estate with a mansion and pleasure gardens but, apart from the barn and cottages, little remains today. Presently swing left and come to a triangular clearing and a three-way junction.

❹ Turn right and climbing, walk beside Waddling Wood which slopes down to Somerleyton Marshes and the river Waveney. In a little over ¼ mile the track bends round to the right, and in a few yards another track coming from a white gate beside the railway joins from the left. Keep straight on and presently, alongside Waveney Grange Farm on the right, arrive at a road on a bend.

❺ Turn left along Station Road, passing a playing field.

❻ The surfaced road ends where a sign points left to Somerleyton Station. Here turn right between long disused wooden gates and climb an earth track. At a waymark, where the track bends right, bear left on a grass path. Very soon swing right and walk through a boat yard, passing a quay on the left. Continue along a gravel road and up a rise to the right. A sign says that this is the Angles Way. Before long meet a track coming in on the right, from the site of the old brickworks.

❼ Eventually reach a road at a telephone box, within sight of the Duke's Head. Turn left, pass the pub on the left and walk along the road, facing the oncoming traffic. Pass on the right Glebe House. Seen half-left, the grey round tower is that of Herringfleet church.

❽ Shortly come to a T-junction. Turn left and in 200 yards pass, on the right, the magnificent barn belonging to the 1655 Manor House Farm. The barn has its date set in its end wall.

❾ Walk on a further 200 yards to see

PLACES of INTEREST

Somerleyton Hall was built in the early 1800s by Sir Morton Peto, a man of tremendous energy and ability. He played a great part in the development of the railways, as well as building many well-known London buildings. The Hall, its gardens and its clipped yew maze are open from Easter till the end of September on Thursdays, Sundays and Bank Holidays. In the months of July and August it is also open on Tuesdays and Wednesdays. The Hall is open from 1.30 pm to 5 pm and the gardens from 12.30 pm to 5.30 pm. Telephone: 01502 730224.

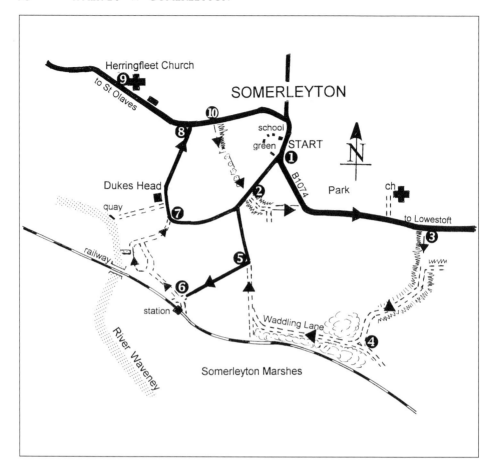

Herringfleet church with its circular tower, somewhat characteristic of Norfolk churches but not common in Suffolk. Now to continue the walk, retrace your steps to the T-junction and go straight on.

⑩ After about 100 yards, passing a long pond on your left, leave the road and go right through a wide gap on the path marked 'Public Footpath to Somerleyton', with a hedge on your left. At the far corner of the field by an electricity pole and a three-way marker turn left for 20 yards and then by an ash tree turn right. Follow the field edge with a line of mature trees on your right. Emerge from the field by wooden half-barriers on to the road and turn left back to the village green.